Behind the Halo

Exploring the Humanity of Jesus

Alice V. Walters

Behind the Halo: Exploring the Humanity of Jesus by Alice V. Walters

Copyright @ 2021 Alice V. Walters

All rights reserved. No part of this publication may be reproduced or transmitted in any form or by any electronic or mechanical means including photo copying, recording, or any information storage and retrieval system now known or to be invented, without permission in writing from the publisher or the author.

Cover design by Robin Black

Cover photo: Cover photo: iStockphoto/francescoch
Author photo: JC Penny Photo Studio, Lifetouch Portrait Studios Inc., 11000 Viking Dr., Suite 200, Eden Prairie, MN. Digital photo used with permission by author.

Scripture quotations from the *Contemporary English Version* (CEV) are Copyright © 1991, 1992, 1995 by American Bible Society. Used by Permission.

Good News Translation® (Today's English Version, Second Edition) Copyright © 1992 American Bible Society. All rights reserved.

The Holy Bible, International Children's Bible® Copyright© 1986, 1988, 1999, 2015 by Tommy Nelson™, a division of Thomas Nelson. Used by permission.

Scripture quotations marked from *The Living Bible* (TLB) are copyright © 1971. Used by permission of Tyndale House Publishers, Carol Stream, Illinois 60188. All rights reserved.

Scripture quotations marked from THE MESSAGE (MSG), copyright © 1993, 2002, 2018 by Eugene H. Peterson. Used by permission of NavPress, represented by Tyndale House Publishers. All rights reserved.

Scripture quotations from.*The New Testament for Everyone.*(NTE) are copyright © Nicholas Thomas Wright 2011.

The Passion Translation®. Copyright © 2017, 2018, 2020 by Passion & Fire Ministries, Inc. Used by permission. All rights reserved..thePassionTranslation.com

Scriptures from the *Revised Standard Version of the Bible* (RSV), copyright © 1946, 1952,.and 1971 National Council of the Churches of Christ in the United States of America. Used by.permission. All rights reserved worldwide.

The Voice Bible, Copyright © 2012 Thomas Nelson, Inc. *The Voice*™ translation © 2012 Ecclesia Bible Society All rights reserved.

Behind the Halo: Exploring the Humanity of Jesus by Alice V. Walters
ISBN: 978-1-952369-91-9
LCCN: 2021912956

Subjects: 1. BODY, MIND, & SPIRIT/Inspiration & Personal Growth
2. FICTION/Historical
3. RELIGION/Christian Living/ Personal Growth

Published by EA Books Publishing, a division of
Living Parables of Central Florida, Inc. a 501c3
EABooksPublishing.com

Dedication

To J.W. & K.V.
I pray each of you finds the One
you are looking for.

Acknowledgments

I've felt like an outsider in my world for most of my life. It took a few decades to accept it. By then I'd built a seemingly impenetrable fortress around me. And then God did that thing He does . . . He bursts through our barriers with love, grace, and laughter.

These are the people the Lord brought with Him as He lovingly forced me to open myself up, to be vulnerable, to share what I'd never said out loud.

Behind the Halo wouldn't have been possible without my publisher, Cheri Cowell. Sitting at a tiny table in an Orlando coffee shop, Cheri exuded confidence in my writing and me. I told her writing dreams that I don't think I'd ever said to another person. All the way through this journey, it's felt like Cheri was my personal cheerleader. I'm so thankful God brought us together.

My Beta Team, Cindy, Sondra, Debbie, and Patty didn't really know what they were taking on when they agreed to walk, and read, alongside me. Not only did they walk and read with me, they pushed me to run and reach farther than I imagined. Thank you, Sisters in Christ, for opening your lives to me, and loving me when I shared mine with you. (Sharing warm soup and laughter were icing on the cake!)

A happy by-product of our Beta Team gatherings was meeting Jana, who became my marketing and technology coach. Her youth, vitality, and expertise brought me to tears more than once, and there was probably some screaming (at least in my head) along the way as Jana pushed me way beyond my comfort zone. That said, more than once I told Jana if I'd had, or been, the kind of inspiring teacher she is, there would have been a lot more learning going on. And just because the Lord likes to show out sometimes, He also blessed me with a new Sister in Christ.

This mama is so proud and blessed that my daughter, Mary, lives and breathes in the literary world. As both writer and editor, she keeps plenty busy, and still took time to edit *Behind the Halo*. Mary's heart and eyes are so finely tuned, she caught and questioned things I had zoomed right past. Nevertheless, Mary used her grace and my gaffs to teach her mom a few new things about writing.

I frequently tell my husband, Tom, that he will need a little red wagon when he gets to heaven to carry all the crowns he's earned on earth to the Throne of Grace, just by living with me. Somewhere during our journey together, Tom learned the delicate balancing act of giving me autonomy and support when it comes to writing, and so many other areas. Trust me, he is much better at it than me, just ask our kids. And on the days when I'm about to melt into a hot mess, my mantra is, "(crisis of the moment) sucks, but Tom loves me." The Lord picked out the perfect Man of God to give me a tangible example of just how far He will go to show His love to me. Dear Reader, I pray there's someone in your life who loves you the same way.

Table of Contents

Acknowledgments v

Introduction ix

At the River .... Matthew 3:13–17 1

Moving Forward .... Luke 4:1–13 5

Hitching a Ride .... Luke 5:1–4 11

Gone Fishing .... Luke 5:4–11 15

Between a Rock and a Hard Place John 2:1–12 19

Out of Control .... John 2:13 – 17 25

Where Do You Get This Stuff .... John 3:1–7, 16–17 31

Unquenchable Thirst .... John 4:4–32 37

The Touch .... Mark 1:21–31 43

That's What Friends Are For .... Luke 5:17–26 49

Paid in Full .... Matthew 9:9–13 57

Calm in the Storm .... Mark 4:35–40 65

Mob Mentality .... Luke 8:26–39 73

You Can't Go Home Again .... Mark 6:1–6 81

It's Time for Lunch .... Luke 6:1–5 87

The Jesus Connection	Matthew 14:22–33	93
What Were You Thinking?	Mark 8:27–28	99
Extravagant Love	Luke 7:37–38	107
Mustard Seeds and Mountains	Matthew 17:14–17	113
The Ones Who Get It	Mark 10:13–16	119
All That Money Can Buy	Mark 10:17–25	123
Can't Keep a Good Man Down!	Mark 10:46–52	129
Come Out!	John 11:32–44	135
Don't Cry for Me	Luke 19:41–44	143
Stay in Your Lane	John 13:1, 3–5. 12–20	147
Deserted	Mark 15:29–34	151
Mother's Day	John 19:25–27	155
Ticket to Paradise	Luke 23:39–43	159
Missing in Action	John 20:11–16	163
Here in the Flesh	Luke 24:36–43	167
Breakfast of Champions	John 21:3–7, 9–12	173
A Fresh Start	John 21:15–17	177
Epilogue		181

Introduction

It's easy to feel comfortable with the two-dimensional Jesus depicted in works of art and Sunday school lessons. Maybe too easy. Maybe so easy that we gloss over or simply dismiss him. But what if we pulled back the curtain?

What if we really got our brave on and considered the man of flesh and blood? I'm not talking about the One touted as being immortal, invincible, all-powerful. What if we looked beyond the divinity of Jesus? What would we see if we looked closer at his interpersonal relationships? Would we see a person who has the same messy, mixed-up emotions as us?

Suppose we considered the One who chose not to live in an ivory tower among priests, prophets, or philosophers, but the man, Jesus, who chose to live among people like us. You know, the IRS worker, some guys from the fishing industry, a woman of wealth, a political activist, retail workers, the wife of a man working for a high-ranking government official. And let's don't forget soldiers, the disabled, the homeless, and other marginalized people.

What if we took off the lens of the cute baby Jesus in storefront manger scenes or the tortured victim of epic Hollywood films? What if we took a minute to see the humanity in Jesus? If we set the trappings of divinity aside, would we see a person who experienced the same feelings and emotions we do? And in doing so, would we discover a connection to the man called Jesus we never realized was possible?

Cast of Characters

- **Jesus:** son of Mary and Joseph; a carpenter by trade; an itinerant teacher by calling
- **Followers:**
  - **Peter and Andrew:** brothers, formerly fishermen
  - **James and John:** brothers, formerly fisherman
  - **Judas Iscariot:** treasurer for band of disciples; some Scriptures recorded that he stole from group coffers
  - **Matthew:** former tax collector
  - **Philip and Nathaniel:** neighbors of Peter and Andrew
  - **Simon (the Zealot):** political activist
  - **Jude and James (the Lesser):** brothers from Galilee
  - **Thomas:** assertive, not afraid to ask hard questions or speak his mind
- **John the Baptist:** itinerant preacher, cousin of Jesus, foretold of Jesus's ministry
- **Pharisees:** Law of Moses bureaucrats
- **Scribes:** students and copyists of scriptures, who sometimes embellished it with their own ideas or traditions
- **Jews:** those belonging to faith community and culture of Abraham and Moses
- **Romans:** ruling force in ancient Middle East

At the River

His dusty feet follow the harsh voice cranked up to fever pitch in the distance. He knows the preacher's voice by reputation and by blood. The traveler quietly chuckles to himself, thinking how surprised his cousin will be. Then the traveler praises God for this man who is willing to sacrifice everything in order to be his herald. A shadow dips and runs across the traveler's face as he glimpses his cousin's ultimate sacrifice for doing God's will.

The faces and feet of people seeking encouragement and hope join the traveler as they all draw closer to the voice in the wilderness. Their hearts are hungry, their hands empty. Inwardly, a glimmer of a smile takes seed in the traveler. The growing crowd's seeking hearts are fertile soil for the message of the preacher, and for the gift only the traveler can give.

Those walking closest to him notice how his shoulders straighten and his head turns upward. Strange behavior in the heat of the day, under the sun that penetrates deep into you, creating a thirst that can't be satisfied. Stranger still, the traveler looks straight up with a smile teasing the corners of his chapped lips. As the voice of the preacher becomes a face then a man, the feet of those starving for his message quicken their paces.

The preacher's eyes seek a place to rest among the many who are already gathered along the banks of the river. He looks at each seeker as if he is the only one around. The preacher who came to show how they can be cleansed of their sins seems to understand what lies deep within each man and each woman. Laid bare are the ugly, the dark, the desperation...the hope without reason or promise. The preacher reaches out a rough, brown hand and tells each one that comes to the water that hope lies in repentance, and in The One to Come.

The One to Come, the traveler, slowly squats down among the crowd, then leans against a rock to lovingly gaze at those around him. A tear escapes his eye as he watches them. One by one they hesitantly creep to the shore. He watches with devotion, and something like pride, as they succumb to the blessing of being cleansed, of going down into a pool of grace and coming up forgiven. Each baptism of faith, each symbolic gesture of dying to sin and being raised to new life, affirms the calling on The One to Come.

It's nearly time. The starving souls surrounding The One to Come hardly notice him. The One to Come slowly stands and slightly shrugs, as if putting off a cloak. He bows his head for a single moment then looks toward the voice of the preacher . . . his cousin . . . his friend. It's time.

The raspy voice and rough hand find completion in the one they're ministering to. With no uncertainty, no guile, the preacher looks at The One to Come, falling to his knees, hitting rock and sand, and cool, soothing water. His hands launch into the air as his face explodes with pure joy.

"My Lord! You have come!" The preacher's voice has become that of a seeker.

"Yes, I've come, just as you told them I would. You've been faithful, John."

"Lord, I'm not worthy to be called your servant. Wash me and cleanse me, oh Lord, from all unrighteousness. For your sake, not mine," John implores his cousin, his friend, The One to Come.

"No, John. It isn't for me to baptize you. You have been washed and made clean by our Father, who is in Heaven."

"Lord, what is your will?"

"Baptize me, John, for through my obedience men will repent and become sons of our heavenly Father."

"But, Lord, I'm not worthy…"

"Baptize me, John, in the name of the Father, and the Son, and the Holy Spirit."

Coarse, calloused hands gently cradle the holy head and shoulders that would bear the sins of the world. Deliberately, with eyes never leaving the face of The One to Come, who came to seek and to save, John lowers him into the muddy waters of sin.

With a shout and a tear, John's arms fall from that sacred head as The One to Come rises with triumph over Satan, sin, and death. The scene of baptism foreshadows his death and resurrection, and will become an outward gesture by those who choose to follow The One to Come.

As a blindingly white dove descends upon him, and a voice, strong and loud and sweet, calls his name, The One to Come, who came to save, laughs out loud, knowing with all certainty that the Father lives in him and he lives in the Father.

BIBLE REFERENCE: Matthew 3:13–17 (Contemporary English Version)

13 Jesus left Galilee and went to the Jordan River to be baptized by John. **14** But John kept objecting and said, "I ought to be baptized by you. Why have you come to me?"

15 Jesus answered, "For now this is how it should be, because we must do all that God wants us to do." Then John agreed.

16 So Jesus was baptized. And as soon as he came out of the water, the sky opened, and he saw the Spirit of God coming down on him like a dove. **17** Then a voice from heaven said, "This is my own dear Son, and I am pleased with him."

Think about a time when a choice brought you great joy or satisfaction. Describe how your choice impacted on your life.

Moving Forward

Jesus, The One to Come, felt like he was in a state of continual motion, always moving. Moving through the crowd and toward John. The waters moving around and over him. The One to Come, full of grace, full of the Holy Spirit, is still moving. Moving toward something, or is it away from something? There is a force compelling him to keep moving…there, in the distance, a vast, deserted place that at first seems void of any life.

The air has become as silent as the stones that bruise his feet through worn sandals. No stirring of life, only the sound of his own movement hanging in the air. No heartbeat in the smallest creature's breast. No breath, fierce and hot, bearing down upon its prey. Nothing. Night and day merge into raging blindness, impotent deafness. What is this place? Why is he here? Why does he feel alone, deserted? Why has his Father's voice faded to a whisper, then to silence?

Moving, drifting, pulled forward…forward to what? *Something's there, but what? A blanket, a pall has fallen, a pall as dark and sinister as a cold night wind. What's out there? What calls to me in my innermost self, my spirit?*

There's a gnawing in his belly. It distracts, penetrating both mind and body. How to satisfy it, pacify it, be rid of it? The accuser's taunts float on the air around him, "The stones, the stones...the stones can become the bread your body craves. All you have to do is say the word . . . the stones can feed you."

Corrosive hunger eats away at his belly, at his brain. Stones? The stones? Perhaps...maybe?

At last, his heavenly Father ignites a spark in Jesus and comforts him, "No, not the stones. They only tear and sink and bruise. There is something greater."

Jesus, The One to Come, shakes his head as if waking up from a deep sleep. *Is that a tree blooming in the distance? This place is here for the conquering. It begs for a champion and entices with false promises of power and submission. I must beware . . . stay alert. The accuser is sinister and diabolical . . . conniving above all else.*

There it is again. The whisper of the accuser slithers around his very being, taunting Jesus again, "Come, I can give you absolute authority if only you'll submit to me. Submit to me and I'll give you the world."

The One to Come feels a touch on his sweaty brow, cool and light as dew. Jesus senses the voice of his heavenly Father. "Can authority be measured in time and space? Can the world be given except by its Creator? Who is worthy of your praise— the creation, or the Creator?"

Looking up, straining onward, Jesus shakes off the taunts of the accuser. Moving, moving again...moving forward, until finally each step becomes lighter, faster than the last. The tree in the distance shows itself to be the entrance to a garden, ripe and full. *Is it the garden, or the tree, or something else that calls? The garden, full of splendor, beckons, but is there more?*

Again, mockery of the accuser fills his ears, "Come, come and see. It's just a little higher, only a little further. Besides, if you stumble, you'll not be bruised. Come and see, test your strength, you cannot fail."

Temptations of the accuser, and weakness of his starving body and spirit batter The One to Come. The blazing heat casts dancing mirages before his eyes, causing him to stumble and fall to his knees. Weariness threatens to destroy him.

But it doesn't. Strength bubbles up inside him. His Father draws him to his feet as His words soothe and empower His son traveling through the wilderness, "You merely stumbled. See? There are no bruises or broken skin. You didn't cry out for help because you didn't need to. I'm as close as your breath, as personal as your heartbeat. My Word is like a cloak you wear about you, always present to protect and guide."

Pulling himself up to his full height, Jesus takes a deep breath, and confronts the one who has tempted and taunted him, "Who do you think you are? If you really knew God's Word, you'd know it says that He is not to be tempted. Obviously, you didn't know whom you were dealing with. You have tried and failed; you have no power over me. There is no place for you here!"

A cooling breeze, a dense carpet of soft, sweet grass, the rush of water tripping over pebbles. A thousand heartbeats, a thousand songs and rhythms. Jesus, The One to Come is invited to a place of peace and strength that can only be found through the Father.

His spirit soars heavenward with a throat full of adoration and praise. His every fiber senses movement all around. Sights and sounds, swirling into a vibrant song of life. The One to Come has trusted and leaned into his Father's loving arms. He was never deserted. He can always count on his heavenly Father to send the Holy Spirit, the Encourager, whenever, wherever he is needed. Joy fills his heart and laughter spills from his lips in triumph over the accuser and tormentor.

BIBLE REFERENCE: Luke 4:1–13 (Revised Standard Version)

1 Now filled with the Holy Spirit, Jesus returned from the Jordan River. And then the Spirit led him into the desert. **2** There the devil tempted Jesus for 40 days. Jesus ate nothing during this time, and when it was finished, he was very hungry.

3 The devil said to him, "If you are the Son of God, tell this rock to become bread."

4 Jesus answered, "The Scriptures say,

'It is not just bread that keeps people alive.'"

5 Then the devil took Jesus and in a moment of time showed him all the kingdoms of the world. **6** The devil said to him, "I will make you king over all these places. You'll have power over them, and you'll get all the glory. It has all been given to me. I can give it to anyone I want. **7** I will give it all to you, if you'll only worship me."

8 Jesus answered, "The Scriptures say,

'You must worship the Lord your God. Serve only him.'"

9 Then the devil led Jesus to Jerusalem and put him on a high place at the edge of the Temple area. He said to him, "If you are the Son of God, jump off! **10** The Scriptures say,

'God will command his angels to take care of you.'

11 It is also written,

*'Their hands will catch you so that
you'll not hit your foot on a rock.'"*

12 Jesus answered, "But the Scriptures also say, 'You must not test the Lord your God.'"
13 The devil finished tempting Jesus in every way and went away to wait until a better time.

---

*Have you ever felt disoriented, out of place?
How did you get grounded again?*

Hitching a Ride

Hungry. The people are all so hungry. How can I give them the encouragement they need when this human body of mine nearly suffocates the spirit within me? But how can I turn away from them? They're my Father's children, my brothers and sisters. Their hearts, their hands, their eyes say they need the bread only I can give.

But this human body! It stumbles and gripes, and rarely does what it's told. How can they bear this flesh? This human frame screams for air and space, but how can I leave them? How can I stay? Shall this frail body convulse into the sea and drown?

Frustration dogged Jesus's thoughts, until he turned to his heavenly Father in prayer for solace and relief.

"Father, forgive my short-sightedness and faint heart. You always provide a means to your end. They mistake my laughter of surprise and relief for rejection of their greatest longings. If only they knew my reliance on you is what empowers me to minister to them.

Why didn't I see the boats before? How could I overlook the fishermen's tired and troubled faces? Forgive me, Father. I know you are the Creator of divine appointments, not chance meetings. We are all here at this time to serve your purpose."

The dialogue in his heart and mind never ceased. It was only through the constant conversation that Jesus was able to complete the tasks he had been given by the Father.

Approaching one of the fishermen, Jesus said, "Simon, do you mind if I sit in your boat for a while? The shore seems to be running out of room before the crowd runs out of needs. Don't worry, I'm just going to sit here and chat with the people for a bit."

"How do you know my name? Why do you want to sit in my boat when there are many others along the shore? Do I know you?" Simon asked, caution spilling over like a cup of water crashing to the floor.

"You don't know me yet, Simon, but sit with me and rest a while. I know you're tired and frustrated from the long night of fishing with nothing to show. It will be all right. Just sit and rest for now."

"How can I sit and rest when there's work to be done? And why do you smile at me?"

"Simon, my joy comes from knowing our heavenly Father longs to give us rest and comfort while our human brains resist him. I'm laughing at myself as well. Please, Simon, you'll understand soon. For now, sit, feel the lull of the waves as you listen to them lap against the shore."

"But sir . . . . "

"Sit, Simon."

Simon reluctantly took his seat in the boat as the crowds settled along the edges of the water, and Jesus took a moment to prepare and focus his spirit by turning again to his Father.

"Father, there must be a big plan for this stubborn man. Thank you for giving him into my charge. As I seek and minister to his needs, I pray he will learn how to seek and minister to the needs of those around him.

"The crowds are still there. There with the water grabbing their cloaks and washing their feet. They're still longing, still hoping I will satisfy their deepest longings and hoping I can wash away the sins and guilt of their souls.

"Thank you, Father! Thank you for loving them. Thank you for trusting me with your children. You are amazing and delightful, and your arms open and ready to welcome. Use me now to pour out your loving, cleansing words to your children!"

BIBLE REFERENCE: Luke 5:1–4 Good News Translation

One day Jesus was standing on the shore of Lake Gennesaret while the people pushed their way up to him to listen to the word of God. **2** He saw two boats pulled up on the beach; the fishermen had left them and were washing the nets. **3** Jesus got into one of the boats—it belonged to Simon—and asked him to push off a little from the shore. Jesus sat in the boat and taught the crowd.

4 When he finished speaking, he said to Simon, "Push the boat out further to the deep water, and you and your partners let down your nets for a catch."

*Sometimes people are just tough nuts to crack.
What tricks do you use to get through to them?*

Gone Fishing

"Andrew, what do you think about John's talk of repentance?"

"All I know is that no matter how hard I try to be all the Pharisees say I should be and do, according to the law of Moses, I never quite measure up. It seems the harder I try, the bigger and deeper the hole in my gut gets."

"Do you think repentance is really the answer? Could it be as easy as confessing our failings, asking for forgiveness, and moving on?"

"I don't know. There's got to be more to life than fishing, sometimes not even catching enough for breakfast, much less to sell. Fishing and a growing sense of failure."

"John says there's someone coming after him. Someone who will take away the sins of the world. Our people have waited generations for a Savior. Do you think we would recognize him if we saw him?"

"I don't know, but for now the guy getting out of Simon's boat seems to want our attention. What was he doing with Simon?"

"Why don't you go see what he wants while I finish cleaning this net?"

Tired and hungry, Andrew trudged to the stranger, who seemed to be smiling like he knew him.

Simon watched the exchange as he finished dragging his boat onto shore. He was still discouraged by another night's work with nothing to show despite the stranger's words to him and the people who had gathered around his boat. Too much to figure out. Like how could he give a tithe to the temple if there was nothing to tithe? Failure. Failure from within, failure from without. Is this all there is to life?

Deep in thought, Simon didn't see Andrew approach, chuckling and shaking his head. "You're never going to believe this! The man talks like he knows us, and says to put the boats out again and throw the nets on the other side."

"He told me the same thing. Told me he knew we'd already fished all night for nothing. Doesn't he have anything better to do than stalk fishermen and make promises to sick and broken people?" Simon grumbled.

"Yeah, yeah. I know, but there was something about him, something in his voice, in his eyes when he looked at me," Andrew answered, looking toward the stranger and rubbing his beard.

"I can't believe I'm saying this, but let's give it a try. What do we have to lose?" Simon asked, already pushing his boat back toward the water.

The face on the shore grew dimmer and dimmer as the fishermen rowed further and further out to sea. They couldn't see his face beaming, or hear the chuckle brewing in his chest, as he prayed.

"Thank you, Father. Thank you for the men you sent me. Thank you for their obedience, for the faith that comes before trust, and for the harvest of souls they will bring into your Kingdom," Jesus prayed, then shaded his eyes to look at the fishermen in the bright morning light.

"Pull, Simon, pull! I've never seen so many fish! Where did they come from?" Andrew bellowed.

"I don't know! I'm just thankful for the harvest and thankful we listened to the man. What did you say his name is?"

"Jesus, I think. Look, he's still on the shore. Wonder what he's waiting for. Maybe he wants a portion of the catch."

The men's voices dwindled down to silence as they strained to bring up net after net full of fish. Soon the boats could hold no more, and the waves seemed to propel them to the shore.

The man, Jesus, who never left the shore, whose eyes never left Andrew and Simon, waited for them. As they pulled the listing boats onto land, they quickly saw and heard Jesus clap his hands and laugh out loud, like a child with a new toy.

"Well done, my sons, well done!"

"Thank you, and thanks for the advice. Our families can eat for weeks now!"

"Andrew, Simon, catching the fish wasn't amazing," he chuckled. "Your amazing obedience brings joy to our Father's heart. Come with me. There is more to life. Come, and I'll make you fishers of men!"

BIBLE REFERENCE: Luke 5:4–11 The Message

4 When he finished teaching, he said to Simon, "Push out into deep water and let your nets out for a catch."

5–7 Simon said, "Master, we've been fishing hard all night and haven't caught even a minnow. But if you say so, I'll let out the nets." It was no sooner said than done—a huge haul of fish, straining the nets past capacity. They waved to their partners in the other boat to come help them. They filled both boats, nearly swamping them with the catch.

8–10 Simon Peter, when he saw it, fell to his knees before Jesus. "Master, leave. I'm a sinner and can't handle this holiness. Leave me to myself." When they pulled in that catch of fish, awe overwhelmed Simon and everyone with him. It was the same with James and John, Zebedee's sons, coworkers with Simon.

10–11 Jesus said to Simon, "There is nothing to fear. From now on you'll be fishing for men and women. And Simon, I think you've already outgrown your name. I'm going to call you "Peter" from now on." After one quick look around them, Andrew and Simon, now Peter, pulled their boats up on the beach, left them, nets and all, and followed Jesus.

---

*Some advice is better than others.
Think about a time following someone's advice
turned out far better than imagined.*

Between a Rock and a Hard Place

"Mom, come on! We're only going to Cana for a few days, not months. You don't have to take everything in the house," Jesus said, following Mary around the house as she continued to add things to a basket.

"I know, Jesus, I know, but you never know what you might need on a journey."

"Mom, really? The guys are all ready to go. Food baskets, bedrolls, good tunics—you name it, we got it."

"Of course, you do, Son, but how many of you have hosted a wedding? Something always gets overlooked or forgotten."

"I get it, Mom, but seriously we're not hosting. It's our job to go and have a good time, not make sure there's enough of everything."

"You forget; I've seen the way you and your friends eat. It won't hurt to take a few loaves of bread, some cheese, fish, and a couple of wineskins."

Shaking his head, Jesus said, "Okay, but that's all. There are no hands to carry more than that."

Suddenly the door opened wide. "Jesus, Mary, what are you doing?" Peter, formerly known as Simon, called, glancing around at the bundles stacked on the table, then at Jesus, who just shrugged his shoulders.

Peter went to Mary and lifted the basket from her hands. "Mary, you pack just like my wife and mother-in-law," Peter said gently and began guiding her to the door. "I'm sure your cousin will appreciate your thoughtfulness, but probably not our tardiness if we don't hit the road now."

Peter turned to wink at Jesus, who was grabbing the remaining baskets and bundles.

Other newly called disciples were hunkered down by the road waiting. As Peter, Mary, and Jesus headed toward them, John jumped up. "'Bout time! I was afraid we were going to miss the bride parade. Andrew said this will be his first parade, too."

Andrew had also stood up but was hanging back a bit. Twisting the corner of a bundle, he muttered, "Peter said the bridal procession is a good way to meet girls."

"Peter, is that what you told your brother?" Mary asked, trying to keep a straight face. "I'm betting that's not how you met your wife, is it?"

Peter turned about three shades of red and glared at Andrew.

"Can we get this show on the road? If we wait any longer I may pass out from hunger," James said, picking up bedrolls and hanging them on his shoulders by their ropes.

The small group made the short journey to Cana in no time, laughing and telling stories as the disciples and teacher they had chosen to follow got to know each other.

The following day, after the couple exchanged vows and received blessings under the canopy, Mary visited with cousins, aunts, and neighbors around the banquet room. Half listening to his new disciples, Jesus smiled as he watched his mother. She could make anyone feel comfortable. Mary seemed to have a way of knowing just what those around her needed.

The next couple of days were filled with food and songs. New in-laws swapped childhood stories about the newlyweds, neighbors chiming in occasionally. Children darted in and out, making new friends and looking for stray sweets on their mothers' plates. Evenings were filled with music and dance.

"Jesus, your mom looks upset!" James frantically whispered, nudging Jesus in the side.

Jesus had seen that look before: Mary was on a mission and she wasn't likely to be deterred.

Rising from his place at the table, Jesus was nearly knocked over as Mary hustled toward him.

"Jesus, our host needs your help! You need to come with me quickly." Mary barely stopped to take a breath.

"Sure, Mom, what's going on?"

"Not here!" Mary said, looking around. "Let's step out onto the porch," she urged Jesus, pulling on his sleeve.

When mother and son had made their way through tables, guests, and servants to the porch, Mary continued pulling Jesus away from the door. "Jesus! We're out of wine. You've got to help!"

"What do you want me to do, Mom? Go to the vintner and purchase more wine? We don't have that kind of money," Jesus answered, stretching out his empty hands.

Still holding onto Jesus's sleeve, Mary shook her head. "Of course not! But I want you to take care of this, I don't want my cousin humiliated in front of all these people."

Battling emotions showed all over Jesus's face. *How can she ask this of me? How can I not respond to her plea? It's not like she's asking for herself. But how could the person who has loved me my whole life put me between a rock and a hard place like this?*

Taking in a deep breath, Jesus's back became as stiff and straight as a board. There was no laughter in his eyes now. This was serious business. "It's not time, Mom. Don't you know what you're asking of me? These men have barely committed to following me. They aren't prepared for such an extraordinary gesture. If I change water into wine, it will change our whole dynamic."

A look of determination came over Mary's face. She thrust out her chin, then did an about-face to go back into the house. Dreading what she might do next, Jesus followed her.

Mary turned the corner into the servants' hall, already waving her hands and calling the wine steward to her. Turning to make sure Jesus was right behind her, she said to the steward, "This is my son, Jesus. Do exactly as he tells you."

Before she left Jesus with the wine steward, Mary faced her son, nodded, and gently captured the tear that spilled onto his cheek. He was no longer just her child; now he was so much more.

BIBLE REFERENCE: John 2:1–12 The Passion Translation

1 Now on the third day there was a wedding feast in the Galilean village of Cana, and the mother of Jesus was there. 2–3 Jesus and his disciples were all invited to the banquet, but

with so many guests in attendance, they ran out of wine. And when Mary realized it, she came to him and asked, "They have no wine, *can't you do something about it?"*

4 Jesus replied, "My dear one, don't you understand that if I do this, it won't change anything for you, but it will change everything for me! My hour *of unveiling my power* has not yet come."

5 Mary then went to the servers and told them, "Whatever Jesus tells you, make sure that you do it!"

6 Now there were six stone water pots standing nearby. They were meant to be used for the Jewish washing rituals. Each one held about 20 gallons or more. **7** Jesus came to the servers and told them, "Fill the *pots with water, right up to the very brim."* **8** Then he said, "Now fill your pitchers and take them to the master of ceremonies."

9 And when they poured out their pitcher for the master of ceremonies to sample, the water became wine! When he tasted the water that became wine, the master of ceremonies was impressed. (Although he didn't know where the wine had come from, but the servers knew.) **10** He called the bridegroom over and said to him, "Every host serves his best wine first until everyone has had a cup or two, then he serves the wine of poor quality. But you, my friend, you've reserved the most exquisite wine until now!"

11 This miracle in Cana was the first of the many extraordinary miracles Jesus performed in Galilee. This was a sign revealing his glory, and his disciples believed in him.

12 After this, Jesus, his mother and brothers and his disciples went to Capernaum and stayed there for a few days.

*Think about a time when you were torn
between two loyalties. How did you choose,
and how did your choice affect those relationships?*

Out of Control

The days at the wedding in Cana had mostly been a relaxed time for the teacher and his new followers to get to know each other. At least it started out that way. Jesus hadn't planned on showing his hand so early in game, but his mother, Mary, put him between a rock and a hard place when she asked him to change water into wine to save the host from embarrassment. His new team was bound to have plenty of questions once they hit the road.

Times with family and celebrations might be rare in the days ahead. Now it was time for Jesus and his disciples to leave Mary in Capernaum and head to Jerusalem. Hopefully eighty miles and several days of walking would be a team-building experience for all of them.

"Jesus, please be careful. You know how quickly word travels. By the time you and the guys get to Jerusalem, some people will have already heard about the wine you produced at the wedding," Mary's voice carried an edge to it. Her finger brushing the hair from his eyes and touching his cheek showed her concern for her son and eased the sharpness in her tone.

"Mom, I'm always careful, but more than that, I'm always seeking my Father's will," Jesus said, taking both of Mary's hands in his. "We know this road is going to be hard, and I know you'll worry about me. Please trust me, and God, to do the right thing."

"Come on, Jesus, we need to get going. The walk to Jerusalem will take three or four days, and we want to be sure to get there before Passover begins. Besides, you know it's going to be crowded," Nathaniel said.

"Yeah, Mary, you know we'll do our best to take care of your boy," Peter laughed, throwing an arm around Jesus's shoulders.

Jesus shrugged Peter's arm from his shoulders and turned to gently caress his mother's face. She wrapped her arms around him and for a moment he let himself be a child again. "I love you, Mom," he whispered.

"Okay, enough of this love fest..." Nathaniel stopped, feeling a sharp elbow to his ribs. "Hey! What are you doing, Philip?"

"Trying to show a little respect," Philip said, walking toward their bundles. He slung one on his back and threw another at Nathaniel before he could say anything else.

The journey was a quiet one. Lots of time for brothers, neighbors, and strangers to get to know one another. Miles outside Jerusalem, Jesus and his growing group of disciples joined the growing crowd of foot traffic. Jerusalem was the place to be if at all possible for Passover. Jesus's new disciples weren't surprised when he began making his way toward the Temple.

The calm journey was over. Jesus's face and posture went from relaxed and open to battle-ready in a heartbeat.

"Jesus, what is it?" Philip asked.

"Are you blind, Philip? Can't you see what's going on?" Andrew said, grabbing the bundle Jesus had thrown to the ground.

As Jesus pushed his way toward the steps onto Solomon's porch, part of the courtyard outside the sanctuary of the Temple, he hissed between gritted teeth, "How dare they defile my Father's house?"

Taking advantage of Andrew moving to the side of the road with two bundles, Peter rushed over and dropped the bedrolls he'd been carrying. "Stay here, Andrew!" he called to his brother.

"What? I'm going too!" Andrew called after Peter, who was running toward Jesus.

"Jesus isn't the only one to make a promise to his mother, Andrew!" Peter paused to yell over his shoulder. "Stay put! Philip, come on! Nathaniel, stay with Andrew!"

The pair of disciples had nearly caught up with Jesus when they saw him twisting some twine and pieces of leather into a whip.

"What's he going to do?" Philip tried to ask Peter over the noise of the crowd.

"I think Jesus is about to give a major smack-down to these merchants and thieves!" Peter hollered back.

And he did. Jesus knocked down tables of moneychangers, sending boxes of coins and cages of animals flying, slicing open moneybags to spill on the pavement.

"What do you think you're doing? Get out of my Father's house! Take your greed and filthy money with you!" Merchants scrambled to recover all they could of their day's work, spewing epithets at this seemingly crazed man wielding a whip. "Don't you know the Lord's house is supposed to be a place of prayer, not a den of thieves? How could you jeopardize your right standing in God's eyes for a few coins? Nothing is worth more than God's Word!"

Peter and Philip pushed and shoved through the crowd but couldn't get to Jesus. In a matter of seconds, he'd turned free enterprise into a free-for-all. Moneychangers were trying to snatch and grab all the coins they could, those who had come to worship were huddling on the fringes, and now priests and Pharisees, the Jewish temple leaders, were joining the fray like storm troopers.

"You, Galilean, who are you?" a priest yelled.

"What do you think you're doing? You have no right to disturb the goings-on of Passover," one of the Pharisees hollered and shook his fist.

Jesus whirled around to face the Pharisees, the men supposedly responsible for upholding and teaching God's Law, head on. He stood for a minute while the riot faded away as quickly as it had begun. In a voice, calm and commanding, Jesus said, "I'm sickened and disgusted at the shame you allow to enter my Father's house?"

"What makes you think you can address us in this way?" a Pharisee challenged him with his chest puffed out and chin thrust upwards. "Give us a sign from God that you have a right to say and do these things."

"Destroy this Temple, and I'll raise it again in three days."

"Now we know you're insane! This Temple took nearly fifty years to build."

Shaking his head, Jesus tossed the whip to one side and walked slowly toward his disciples. Peter and Philip seemed to be attached to the steps as he approached.

"Jesus, Jesus, are you okay? That was pretty wild. What were you thinking?" Peter asked as they headed back to where they'd left Andrew and Nathaniel.

"I was thinking there is so much work to be done," Jesus said, stopping in the middle of the road. He turned and looked closely at the men before him. "And I'm thankful for the people my heavenly Father is giving me to get it done.

BIBLE REFERENCE: John 2:13–22 (The Message)

13–14 When the Passover Feast, celebrated each spring by the Jews, was about to take place, Jesus traveled up to Jerusalem. He found the Temple teeming with people selling cattle and sheep and doves. The loan sharks were also there in full strength.

15–17 Jesus put together a whip out of strips of leather and chased them out of the Temple, stampeding the sheep and cattle, upending the tables of the loan sharks, spilling coins left and right. He told the dove merchants, "Get your things out of here! Stop turning my Father's house into a shopping mall!" That's when his disciples remembered the Scripture, "Zeal for your house consumes me."

18–19 But the Jews were upset. They asked, "What credentials can you present to justify this?" Jesus answered, "Tear down this Temple and in three days I'll put it back together."

20–22 They were indignant: "It took forty-six years to build this Temple, and you're going to rebuild it in three days?" But Jesus was talking about his body as the Temple. Later, after he was raised from the dead, his disciples remembered he had said this. They then put two and two together and believed both what was written in Scripture and what Jesus had said.

> *What do you think makes a person*
> *charge headlong into a conflict?*
> *Reflect on a time you ran, or witnessed someone*
> *you knew run, full throttle into danger.*
>
>

Where Do You Get This Stuff?

"Lord, it's been a long day. You need to rest."

"Rest? How can I rest when so many are hurting, are seeking? What about those who only seek what I can do for the flesh, and aren't concerned with their souls?"

"Master," pleaded Philip, "everyone has gone home. How can you minister to anyone tomorrow if you don't rest tonight?"

"Philip, do you remember when I told you I've food to eat that you don't know about?"

"I remember. You said your food is to do the will and the work of your heavenly Father."

Jesus smiled indulgently at his disciple, like a father smiling over his child. Philip seemed to enjoy serving others, but he didn't always see how to overcome obstacles to service.

"That's right, Philip. I also find rest in my heavenly Father, a rest that no bed or pallet can provide."

"But, Lord …"

"It's really all right, Philip. Besides, I'm expecting someone. You go on and find your bed like the others."

"If someone is coming this late at night, maybe I should wait with you."

"You're a good and thoughtful man, Philip, but it's best if I receive this visitor alone. Go to bed. I can tell I'm not the only one who's tired."

"Are you sure, Lord?"

"I'm sure. Now go get some rest. I'm also sure we will have more people to minister to tomorrow."

As Philip slowly walked to the door, Jesus sighed thinking how different his disciples were. Different backgrounds, different personalities, different needs. Sometimes it seemed like meeting their needs, and teaching them to trust God to meet them, was a full-time ministry in itself. And there was never enough time to serve everyone who needed his touch.

Gazing out the window and into the night, Jesus found solace and strength in sharing his thoughts with God as he prayed.

"Father, thank you for each of the men and women you have placed in my care. Thank you for the gifts you have blessed them with, and that they're learning to share with others. Thank you for the countless lives they will touch, and the sacrifices they willingly make. Thank you for patience, wisdom, and discernment as I teach them about your will.

"Father, thank you for the searching heart that is about to arrive. Help me turn his timidity into trust and his faintheartedness to faith in you. Show me your will, Father, that I may bring light into this darkened world."

Deep in conversation with his Father and surrounded by the cool air and darkness that hovered in the room, Jesus didn't immediately hear the man enter, head bowed, feet shuffling.

"Rabbi? Rabbi, may I talk to you?" a frightened voice whispered.

"Nicodemus, I've been expecting you!" Jesus turned and said with the grin of someone who has been looking forward to seeing a good friend.

"Rabbi, I believe you were sent by God. How else could you do these signs and miracles?" Nicodemus's words and questions were leaping from his mouth so quickly he began to stammer.

"You believe in me, but you still have questions," Jesus replied, casually motioning Nicodemus to sit beside him on the bench.

"I'm sorry, Lord," Nicodemus muttered, as he looked away. "As a Pharisee serving on the Sanhedrin, the highest court within the Temple, studying, interpreting, and upholding Scripture is my life. I should have fewer questions and more answers."

"Are you so steeped in prestige and study that you're embarrassed to have questions? Is that why you came to me in the dark?"

Nicodemus shook his head and looked at the floor. "For hundreds of years, our people have looked for, waited for, and hoped for a savior. After a lifetime of hoping and studying, I'm afraid of making a mistake of the gravest consequence."

Smiling, Jesus laid a hand on Nicodemus's arm. "Nicodemus, unless you're born again, experience spiritual birth, you'll not see the kingdom of God that you earnestly long for."

Rubbing his forehead, Nicodemus asked, "How can I be born again?"

"Think, Nicodemus, think. You make this too hard. That which is flesh is flesh, including your physical birth. That which is Spirit, the innermost part of you, is from our heavenly Father."

"I'm trying to understand."

Jesus shook his head and chuckled quietly. "My son, you speak of earthly things you know. I'm trying to teach you things of the Spirit."

Quiet and darkness engulfed the men in the sanctuary from the hectic world outside. Understanding seemed poised and ready to be experienced by the Temple leader. Nicodemus jumped up to pace around the room, rubbing his palms, pulling his beard, while Jesus waited patiently. He would know when Nicodemus was ready for the next step.

Slowly, Nicodemus turned toward the bench where Jesus still sat and dropped to the cool stones of the ledge. Suddenly, Nicodemus seemed to crumble from within. Rising quickly, Jesus moved to his side and placed a strong, but gentle hand upon his shoulder.

"My son, we have much to discuss now that you have surrendered your will to our heavenly Father."

"How did you know, Lord?" Nicodemus slowly raised his head and asked.

"My Father and I are one. He sees and hears what I see and hear, and I do the same with him. We heard what your heart had to say. Now it's time for you to hear what we have to say."

"I've so much to learn. How could I be so blind . . . so ignorant? I must seem very foolish to you, Master."

"Fools choose to remain ignorant, Nicodemus. Do I speak to you as a fool or as the scholar you are?"

"Forgive me, Lord. I want to understand what you're trying to teach me. Honestly, I do. But years of training clutter my brain."

"Let these words comfort your heart. God loves the world so much He is willing to give his own child for it. Those who believe in him, in me, have eternal life. I didn't come to judge and condemn the world. **I came for you!**" Jesus grinned at the Pharisee.

Jesus paused to allow his words to soak into the very fiber of Nicodemus's being. Then he watched a parade of emotions and expressions chase each other across the Pharisee's face. Finally, as a look of wonder followed by acceptance settled into place, Jesus threw back his head as a throaty chuckle exploded into joyous laughter.

"My Lord, how could you love me so?" Nicodemus's voice hinted at his amazement.

"Don't wonder at my love for you, Nicodemus. Wonder that there are those who choose their iniquity, their lives of sin, over the love the Father and I have for them."

The teacher and pupil sat in comfortable silence for a time. As evening breezes waned and the morning star began to rise, Jesus also rose.

"There is much work to do, Nicodemus. Work that you'll have a part in. Return to your home, and your studies, and your duties. You'll know what to do and when to do it."

"I came to question a rabbi, but I'm leaving knowing my Savior," Nicodemus said, hugging Jesus in farewell.

BIBLE REFERENCE: John 3:1–7, 16–17 International Children's Bible

1 There was a man named Nicodemus who was one of the Pharisees. He was an important Jewish leader. **2** One night Nicodemus came to Jesus. He said, "Teacher, we know that you're a teacher sent from God. No one can do the miracles you do, unless God is with him."

3 Jesus answered, "I tell you the truth. Unless you are born again, you cannot be in God's kingdom."

4 Nicodemus said, "But if a man is already old, how can he be born again? He cannot enter his mother's body again. So how can he be born a second time?"

5 But Jesus answered, "I tell you the truth. Unless you are born from water and the Spirit, you cannot enter God's kingdom. **6** A person's body is born from his human parents. But a person's spiritual life is born from the Spirit. **7** Don't be surprised when I tell you, 'You must all be born again'..

16 "For God loved the world so much that he gave his only Son. God gave his Son so that whoever believes in him may not be lost, but have eternal life. **17** God did not send his Son into the world to judge the world guilty, but to save the world through him."

---

*Think about a time when you just didn't get it.
Maybe on the job, learning a new skill, in a relationship.
How did you know when it clicked? How did you feel
when it all suddenly made sense?*

Unquenchable Thirst

Jesus was tired, tired from healing, tired from preaching, tired from giving all he had and still never feeling like it was enough.

He was relieved to send the disciples into town on the pretense of getting him something to eat. You'd think by now they would start to understand his only sources of rest and refreshment came from spending time with his heavenly Father.

Wrapped in solitude, Jesus immersed himself in the power of fellowship with his Father. Once again, he was able to draw a sense of meaning and purpose, remembering success is measured on a heavenly scale, not one determined by man.

A sense of peace and strength saturated the teacher as he leaned against a tree near the well. He allowed the Father to restore his soul as he prepared for his next encounter. In this earthly shell, he sometimes waffled between wonder at the tasks he'd been given, and the enormity of them.

Jesus clung to his Father's promise to never leave or forsake him. He knew the Father would guide him through the conversation with the woman approaching if he sought to do the Father's will, and not his own.

As the woman drew near to the well, he said to her, "Would you give me a drink?"

The woman laughed out loud, her voice dripping with resentment, "Why would a Jew ask a Samaritan woman for a drink? You don't usually bother with us."

Now it was Jesus's turn to laugh, but with mercy and tolerance as a parent would while watching a wayward child. "If you knew who was asking for water, you would have asked me instead."

"What are you talking about? You have nothing to draw the water from the well, Sir, so how can you offer me water? This well was given to us by our father, Jacob. He and his family and his animals drank from this well. Are you better than Jacob that you can offer something with no way to give it?"

"The water of this well will never quench your thirst. Mine will take away your thirst forever, and will bubble up inside you to quench your every longing."

"That sounds wonderful! Please give me this water so I may never thirst again or have to come to the well to draw water," the woman said, putting her jar down and her hand on her hip.

As the woman glared at the teacher, he saw her look of arrogance melt into a pool of shame. A woman didn't come to the well alone at midday, only an outcast. Jesus looked within to see her pain and hunger, masked by a thin veil of brazenness. Knowing her passage from hurt to holy could be accomplished only through repentance and forgiveness, the teacher pressed on.

"Go get your husband and come back."

"Husband? I don't have a husband."

"That's true, you don't have a husband right now. You've had five husbands, and the man you're currently living with isn't your husband."

Realizing this man had her figured out, and still continued to talk to her, the Samaritan woman dropped to his feet. "I get it now; you're a prophet. Our fathers have worshipped on this mountain, but you Jews say we should go to Jerusalem to worship. Why do you prophesy to me in this place? I don't understand."

Jesus patiently explained to her God's plan to save all His people, and that they would be able to worship Him in spirit, not just in a specific place. The shroud of shame and misconception that was draped around the woman ripped in two. Jesus smiled as her face showed her slowly grabbing hold of what he was telling her.

"I know a Savior has been promised to us, one who will tell us everything we need to know and make sure we understand it clearly," she said, in a voice barely above a whisper.

As the light in the woman's face grew, a chuckle in Jesus's throat grew into laughter. "You do see! I'm The One to Come that you have been waiting for. **I came for you!**"

Before she could stop herself, the Samaritan woman grasped his legs and wept tears of sorrow and joy. Jesus gently stroked her hair. It was a new person who finally looked up into the face of her Savior.

"You're free!" exalted Jesus, then the two of them laughed out loud in the victory of the heavenly Father's saving grace.

The woman dashed into town to tell her story, just as the disciples were returning from their errand. They grilled Jesus about why he would talk to such a woman. He shook his head, with a lopsided grin on his face, at their lack of understanding. The puzzled disciples finally walked off to prepare the food they'd purchased, their steps slow and hobbled by frustration.

"Come and eat, Master," one of them called.

"I'm full and satisfied," Jesus said, stretching and sprawling on the grass.

The disciples looked at each other and questioned if someone had brought him something to eat while they had been away.

"Don't look so baffled. My food is to do my Father's will, to complete the work he's given me. You consider the time is only for healing the flesh, that people aren't ready to receive forgiveness and salvation. But look around you. There is a harvest of souls to capture for the Kingdom of God here and now."

Jumping up and throwing his arms around two of his followers, Jesus walked to where the food was ready and waiting, chuckling like he was the only one to know the punch line to a joke.

BIBLE REFERENCE: John 4:4–32 The Message

So Jesus left the Judean countryside and went back to Galilee. **4–6** To get there, he had to pass through Samaria. He came into Sychar, a Samaritan village that bordered the field Jacob had given his son Joseph. Jacob's well was still there. Jesus, worn out by the trip, sat down at the well. It was noon.

7–8 A woman, a Samaritan, came to draw water. Jesus said, "Would you give me a drink of water?" (His disciples had gone to the village to buy food for lunch.)

9 The Samaritan woman, taken aback, asked, "How come you, a Jew, are asking me, a Samaritan woman, for a drink?" (Jews in those days wouldn't be caught dead talking to Samaritans.)

10 Jesus answered, "If you knew the generosity of God and who I am, you would be asking *me* for a drink, and I would give you fresh, living water."

11–12 The woman said, "Sir, you don't even have a bucket to draw with, and this well is deep. So how are you going to get this 'living water'? Are you a better man than our ancestor Jacob, who dug this well and drank from it, he and his sons and livestock, and passed it down to us?"

13–14 Jesus said, "Everyone who drinks this water will get thirsty again and again. Anyone who drinks the water I give will never thirst—not ever. The water I give will be an artesian spring within, gushing fountains of endless life."

15 The woman said, "Sir, give me this water so I won't ever get thirsty, won't ever have to come back to this well again!"

16 He said, "Go call your husband and then come back."

17–18 "I have no husband," she said.

"That's nicely put: 'I have no husband.' You've had five husbands, and the man you're living with now isn't even your husband. You spoke the truth there, sure enough."

19–20 "Oh, so you're a prophet! Well, tell me this: Our ancestors worshiped God at this mountain, but you Jews insist that Jerusalem is the only place for worship, right?"

23–24 "It's who you are and the way you live that count before God. Your worship must engage your spirit in the pursuit of truth. That's the kind of people the Father is out looking for: those who are simply and honestly *themselves* before him in their worship. God is sheer being itself—Spirit. Those who worship him must do it out of their very being, their spirits, their true selves, in adoration."

25 The woman said, "I don't know about that. I do know that the Messiah is coming. When he arrives, we'll get the whole story."

26 "I am he," said Jesus. "You don't have to wait any longer or look any further."

27 Just then his disciples came back. They were shocked. They couldn't believe he was talking with that kind of a woman. No one said what they were all thinking, but their faces showed it.

28–30 The woman took the hint and left. In her confusion she left her water pot. Back in the village she told the people, "Come see a man who knew all about the things I did, who knows me inside and out. Do you think this could be the Messiah?" And they went out to see for themselves.

31 In the meantime, the disciples pressed him, "Rabbi, eat. Aren't you going to eat?"

32 He told them, "I have food to eat you know nothing about."

Consider a time you had the opportunity to connect with someone of a cultural background different from your own. How did it better your understanding of God and His children?

The Touch

"Master, are you sure? The temple looks really crowded," the disciple questioned his teacher.

"James, I didn't come for my sake. I came for the sake of the lost, and to bring glory to our heavenly Father. Should I ignore either?" Jesus said, quickening his pace.

"No, Lord. It's just that they don't look very friendly, much less in a mood to bring God glory," James answered.

"In time, you'll learn that His glory isn't of our making; it comes from our obedience to His will. Come on, it's time to be obedient," Jesus assured his follower.

"I still don't like the looks of this," James mumbled, shaking his head.

As the small band of men entered the synagogue, unkempt and unwashed, the Pharisees and Levites, religious leaders in the Temple looked at them in astonishment. How dare these fishermen enter the temple without bathing or getting cleaned up? Who did they think they were?

All of the men, except the One, tried to blend into the walls around them. Jesus, the One, walked confidently to the front of the synagogue, and opening the scrolls, began to proclaim the word of the Lord. Without hesitation, he spoke as one in authority to all who would listen.

As Jesus preached, a man with an unclean spirit came forward and tried to confront him. Jesus wouldn't have any part of the tainted spirit. He chastised the spirit and commanded it to come out from the man. The man was thrown to the floor, in a fit, as the spirit fled from him.

"Jesus, Jesus," Andrew sputtered from his place along the wall. "Quickly, come away. Come away, before they seize you for a sorcerer."

"Yes, Lord, come now. Don't anger the Pharisees. They hold all the cards," Peter added, straining to grab Jesus's sleeve.

Jesus looked from the man slowly rising from the floor, to the Pharisees, and finally to his disciples. The glimmer of a smile dashed across his face as he turned to leave the synagogue, taking the man, now free of the unclean spirit, with him.

The disciples emerged from the shadows, but not before hearing the astonished church leaders gasp at the power and authority that caused them to listen, and the unclean spirit to obey.

Walking quickly to catch up with Jesus and his newest follower, the disciples were surprised to hear him chuckle.

"Lord, don't you see how you aroused their interest, their suspicions?"

"Have I, Peter?"

"Surely you know the laws of Moses, and you know the Pharisees and the Levites are very strict in adherence, for themselves and for everyone else."

"Peter, how can you call me Lord, and not believe in my sovereignty? I tell you the Father is in me, as I am in the Father.

Have you not believed and understood that before Moses and the law, I was?"

"Jesus, we're poor, with hardly any schooling. How can we expect to know and understand all that you tell us?" John asked quietly.

"Simple, John, believe I am who I say I am. Look around. What do you see?"

"I see people who are lonely, and scared, and frustrated," John said, stopping to look closely at the crowd.

"You mean, lost?"

"Jesus, there are so many! What can we do for them?" James asked, holding out empty hands.

Jesus grabbed one of James's hands and threw an arm around John's shoulder to draw the small group of men into a huddle.

"James, John, you have taken the first steps. You see the lost and want to help them, and you want to help them for their sakes, not your own. All of that brings God glory. Isn't that our game plan?"

"Right now, I'm hoping our game plan includes a good meal, and giving my head a little rest," Peter interjected.

"Good thing we're almost home, Peter. I hope there's enough for one more," James said.

"There's always enough for more when our Father blesses it," Jesus told him, placing a hand on his shoulder.

The men finished walking the short distance to Andrew and Peter's house, talking, laughing, and wondering about what they had just witnessed. Fragrant odors of fresh-baked bread, and fresh-caught fish guided them to the door.

Rushing to meet them, Peter's wife told him that her mother had taken sick while they were away. The fever continued, no matter how she tried to relieve it.

Peter tentatively glanced at the man he called Lord.

"Peter, do you believe?"

"I, I don't know. I saw you heal this man with my own eyes. My head says if you can heal him, you can heal my mother-in-law. My heart is afraid to hope," Peter mumbled, tucking his chin into his chest.

"Peter, your honesty blesses you. What I do now is as much for your sake, and the rest of you, as for hers."

As Jesus turned to go to her, the disciples thought they heard him softly chortle. A few minutes later, Peter's mother-in-law was fussing around the fire and putting out bowls for a meal.

While they were finishing the bread and fish, John asked, "Jesus, were you laughing at us earlier?"

"Not exactly, John. Sometimes I forget that faith is new and fragile for you. I laugh at myself for not remembering that you don't see what I see yet, and I laugh about the joys you have yet to experience."

"When will we see what you see, Lord?" John asked, around a mouthful of bread and fish. "And when will we experience these joys you speak of?"

"Our journey is just beginning, John. We will see much together. For now, enjoy the company of our new friend and the hospitality of Peter's family in caring for us," Jesus assured his disciple, passing a bowl of steaming fish and bread to the man healed in the temple.

BIBLE REFERENCE: Mark 1:21–31 Contemporary English Version

23 While Jesus was in the synagogue, a man was there who had an evil spirit inside him. The man shouted, **24** "Jesus of Nazareth! What do you want with us? Did you come to destroy us? I know who you are—God's Holy One!"

25 Jesus, his voice full of warning, said, "Be quiet, and come out of him!" **26** The evil spirit made the man shake. Then the spirit made a loud noise and came out of him.

27 The people were amazed. They asked each other, "What is happening here? This man is teaching something new, and he teaches with authority! He even commands evil spirits, and they obey him." **28** So the news about Jesus spread quickly everywhere in the area of Galilee.

29 Jesus and the followers left the synagogue. They all went with James and John to the home of Simon and Andrew. **30** Simon's mother-in-law was very sick. She was in bed and had a fever. The people there told Jesus about her. **31** So he went to her bed. Jesus held her hand and helped her stand up. The fever left her, and she was healed. Then she began serving them.

> *Have you ever gone against the grain,*
> *bucked the crowd? Recall what happened*
> *and how you explained your actions.*

That's What Friends Are For

"Are you sure this is a good idea?" Malachi's voice sounded as anguished as his face looked. His friends had insisted on carrying his broken body to see a new teacher, they said . . . a charlatan, Malachi feared.

"Of course, we're sure. I told you, we've heard this man, Jesus, preach and we've seen his touch heal others. Don't you believe us?" Nathan grinned at his friend. He was not afraid to speak up whether it was the worst or best circumstances.

"How many hopes and promises for healing have been dashed against the rocks, just as my feet and legs have crumbled and dashed my worthless body against them? I'm tired—tired of disappointment, tired of trying to believe I'll be whole someday, and knowing it's not true," Malachi whined, trying to cover his face with an edge from one of the blankets used to make his pallet. He finally closed his eyes as resignation fell across his face. Gently carrying the pallet, his four friends looked at each other and smiled.

As the small group inched their way toward the house of the preacher and healer, the noise of expectant chatter increased with the size of the crowd.

"Why are you stopping?" moaned Malachi. "Let's just go home."

"Open your eyes! Look! These aren't just people hoping for healing; there are also people who have been healed! They're telling their stories. Here comes one now! Sir, sir? Did you see Jesus?" Josef asked, reaching out to a passing stranger with his free hand.

"See Jesus? See Jesus! Yes, I saw him!" the stranger said. "I saw him with eyes that have only seen blackness until now. With one hand holding mine and his other on my eyes, he touched me and healed me. See Jesus? He opened my eyes and gave me the world. Praise God!"

The man whose sight had just been restored by the teacher practically skipped away, stopping every few steps to share his miracle with someone or simply stare at the world around him.

"Didn't we tell you this man, Jesus, was different?" Jonathan asked Malachi, briefly pausing to adjust the ropes used to carry the bedroll they had turned into a pallet.

"He gave sight to a blind man. Good for both of them. My eyes work just fine, thank you very much. Can we go home now? I can barely breathe with all these people crowding around," Malachi said, shaking his head with disgust and frustration.

"No! We aren't going home until we see Jesus! The way you talk, I'm more concerned about him healing your heart than healing your legs," Jonathan retorted, glaring at Malachi.

"My heart, hah! My heart works about as well as my legs. Why do you even bother with me?"

"Sometimes I wonder, but right now I'm wondering how we're going to get you into the house," Benjamin said, looking around at all the people who had gathered at the house where the teacher was staying.

With the crowd now at a standstill, the friends looked around for options and ideas. They were all beginning to feel discouraged. So many people, all hoping for a few minutes with this man, this healer, this Jesus.

"Do you see the edge around the roof?" asked Josef from his corner of the pallet the friends carried. "I'll bet it's a sleeping roof. If that's the case, some of the roof tiles will lift right off."

"That's great, but how are we going to get up there, then lower Malachi down into the house?" Benjamin asked the question they all had.

"Let's carry him over to the shade, and I'll run home for some rope," Nathan offered.

"Hurry! The sun will start to set soon."

The quartet of men carried their stubborn passenger to the shade of a nearby tree, gently setting him down. Benjamin sat down and leaned against the tree beside Malachi, still lying on his pallet. Jonathan and Josef collapsed onto the cool, soft grass, sprawling in the shade like they didn't have a care in the world. While the air around the men pulsated with hope and healing, the men seemed totally confident and at ease with each other and their mission.

After a few minutes of quiet, Malachi softly cleared his throat and spoke up.

"I've been lying here watching each of you. Even though you have much more important things to do, you're here with me. Josef, who's fishing for you today? Benjamin, I know it's lambing season. Who's tending your ewes?" Malachi took a long, slow breath, and hung his head. "All I've done today is complain, and probably not said a word of thanks."

"That's okay, Malachi. We're glad to be here for you," Benjamin said, reaching over to pat Malachi on the shoulder.

"That's just it, Benjamin. Not only have none of you complained. Instead, you've seemed happy to help me, even more than usual."

"I've been to hear Jesus preach. He said God loves a cheerful giver. When somebody asked him if God loves us when we have nothing to give, Jesus said we all have our hearts, our hands, and our time. He said these are the best gifts we have to offer, and when we give them happily and without hesitation, God smiles." Benjamin said, looking around at his nodding companions.

"Well, he must be smiling pretty big over you four. I'm sorry I've been so selfish. Maybe my miracle today is realizing how much each one of you blesses my life," Malachi told his friends, reaching out to take their hands.

"Did somebody say something about a miracle?" called Nathan, as he came running with rope. "I brought all I had, then went to Josef's house for more."

"Sounds like we have everything we need, willing hands, willing hearts, and plenty of rope. Malachi, are you ready for the rest of your miracle?" asked Josef.

Overwhelmed by the love and devotion of his friends, Malachi could only shake his head, as a tear slid from the corner of one eye.

Jonathan touched Malachi on the shoulder, and said, "Remember, Malachi, let us do the work, Jesus do the healing, and you do the receiving."

Being men who worked with their hands every day, the group of friends made short work of getting Malachi to the roof of the house. Since it was summer, some of the roof tiles were already open to let air into the house, and sleepers onto the roof. They easily removed a few more tiles of the roof and looked down into the gathering. A look of authority and compassion on his face made Jesus easy to spot.

"Jesus, were you expecting a visitation?" called a loud, rough voice from the room below.

"What's that, Peter?" Jesus asked, looking toward his companion.

"It looks like we have visitors from on high. Look at the ceiling, or what's left of it."

As the man called Jesus looked up, a smile burst onto his face. "Malachi, you're here! I've been expecting you and your friends. I'm so happy you made it! "

Looking around the opening in the roof, Jesus smiled even broader. "Benjamin, Nathan, Josef, Jonathan, I knew I could count on you! You have blessed Malachi and me both today!"

The friends eased Malachi down into the room as people separated like the Red Sea. Seekers, who were now onlookers, said later that the men's faces nearly outshone the sun.

"Malachi, I'm so proud of you! It takes a man after God's own heart to repent and seek forgiveness," Jesus encouraged the man on the pallet.

"I haven't been very kind to my friends, Lord, or thankful for what they have done for me. I'm so sorry."

Placing his hand on the lame man's head, Jesus said, "My son, you're already forgiven. Our heavenly Father sees the heart.

He knows when we fail, and when we repent. Remember, he is always ready to forgive those who truly seek him."

Within the crowd, there were those who had come looking for a reason to torment, tempt, or try to disarm the work of this so-called "Son of God". A voice filled with hatred called out, "Blasphemy! Only God can forgive! This man blasphemes! How dare you call him "Lord"?"

One look of authority from Jesus silenced the voice. Turning back to Malachi, who seemed to be folding in on himself, Jesus asked tenderly, "Malachi, are your sins forgiven?"

Afraid to look at him, Malachi shrugged his shoulders.

Kneeling in front of him, Jesus looked into Malachi's eyes, into his heart, and asked again, "Malachi, are your sins forgiven?"

As newborn confidence began to well up within him, Malachi straightened his back, raised his head, and in a voice filled with assurance he looked at Jesus and said, "Yes, Lord, I am forgiven!"

Laughter as loud as a ram's horn burst from Jesus as he rocked back on his heels. "Malachi, you're forgiven and loved by our heavenly Father. Would you also like to walk?"

As Jesus said this, he took Malachi by the hands and slowly raised him to his feet. Malachi's eyes never left Jesus's until Jonathan exclaimed, "Malachi's walking! Praise God, Malachi is walking!"

Once again, the crowd in the house parted like the Red Sea. This time the man picked up and carried his pallet through the crowd to the door, where he turned and laughed out loud with his Lord, then raced to catch up with his friends who had already begun sharing Malachi's story to those waiting outside.

BIBLE REFERENCE: Mark 2:1–12 Revised Standard Version

And when he returned to Caper-na-um after some days, it was reported that he was at home. **2** And many were gathered together, so that there was no longer room for them, not even about the door; and he was preaching the word to them. **3** And they came, bringing to him a paralytic carried by four men. **4** And when they could not get near him because of the crowd, they removed the roof above him; and when they had made an opening, they let down the pallet on which the paralytic lay. **5** And when Jesus saw their faith, he said to the paralytic, "My son, your sins are forgiven." **6** Now some of the scribes were sitting there, questioning in their hearts, **7** "Why does this man speak thus? It is blasphemy! Who can forgive sins but God alone?" **8** And immediately Jesus, perceiving in his spirit that they thus questioned within themselves, said to them, "Why do you question thus in your hearts? **9** Which is easier, to say to the paralytic, 'Your sins are forgiven,' or to say, 'Rise, take up your pallet and walk'? **10** But that you may know that the Son of man has authority on earth to forgive sins"—he said to the paralytic— **11** "I say to you, rise, take up your pallet and go home." **12** And he rose, and immediately took up the pallet and went out before them all; so that they were all amazed and glorified God, saying, "We never saw anything like this!"

What would we do without friends?
Think about times a friend went out of the way to help you,
or when you went out of your way to help a friend.

Paid in Full

Jesus walked quickly down the road, eyes straight ahead. He was obviously on some sort of mission, and focused on accomplishing it.

As he neared the town, people began to join Jesus on the road. Without waiting for each one to stop and tell him their greatest need, physical, spiritual, or mental, one glance told him all he needed to know. Looking ahead, he spotted a clearing with a large shade tree. Making his way to the tree, the pleas, silent and spoken, began to crescendo. Hands, some tentative, too many of them tortured, reached out to him.

"Children, do you see the clearing? Come to the shade. Come to its coolness and protection. Come to me…" Jesus called.

A sense of excitement ignited and spread throughout the crowd who swarmed around Jesus. Their faces seemed to brighten with hope that they would receive the tangible encouragement they desperately sought. Steps were lighter as burdens began to slide from weary shoulders.

"He sees me!" said a hobbling, young husband, leaning on his careworn wife.

A small child clutched her mother's hand and said anxiously, "Mama, I can hear the man. Is he looking at me? Will he help me see?"

A wrinkled, old woman wondered out loud to her companion, "I'm too old. These worries have rotted my soul. What can this man do for me?"

"Sit, children. There is a brook just over there," Jesus waved his arms, beckoning, directing. "Rest... refresh. I know you're tired. I know your burdens are heavy, but I came to give you hope and peace."

Slowly, Jesus made his way among them. He touched a leathery face, looking deep into eyes filled with time and torment, and watched the shroud be lifted. A mother lovingly lifted her child toward him, and he gladly took the girl into his arms. Laughter trickled up his throat and into the mouth of the child until he returned her to her mother, eyes wide open and gazing at the world around her. He reached out to the young husband, who stood, unattended for the first time since the ox had stumbled and fallen on him with the plow.

One by one, he reached for, touched, and healed them. His soul grew heavy from the burdens they feebly tried to carry, until he thanked his heavenly Father that he was here, and they had come.

Some solemn, some exuberant, all amazed, all healed, they hesitantly drifted toward their homes. How could they repay him? How could they thank Jesus and tell him how he had changed their lives? One look at Jesus's gentle face and the almost imperceptible nod told each one he knew, he understood.

Jesus calmly sat and leaned against the tree. He lifted his face as if to drink in the coolness of the shade, or was it something else? Tranquility glided across his face until it was overtaken by a look of resolution. With a stretch, a sigh, and a shrug, he drifted to his feet and gazed down the road to his next encounter.

Approaching the city, heat and humanity grew. As Jesus deliberately made his way and began to wind his way through the streets of businesses and trading, he didn't seem to notice the pounding sun or crowd. Instead, he focused on one area teeming with hostility. He stepped off the road and paused for a few minutes, watching and listening to the exchanges, verbal and monetary.

As greed exacted its toll, coins sparkled and splashed into gold-plated coffers. Harsh words overtook and overpowered humble ones of acquiescence. Known for their greed and association with the Roman enemy, Jewish tax collectors harbored no false notions of acceptance. They had made their choices to trade fealty for finery, and most were satisfied with that.

Jesus watched briefly, unnoticed because of his clothing and presumed station in life, then gradually eased into the tax line. He knew the one he had come for. He knew this tax collector's calculating heart, and he knew his affection for full coffers. Jesus also knew the darkest nights can foretell the brightest dawn.

"Where's your bill?" a coarse voice finally broke into his thoughts. "How much do you owe?" the gruff speaker continued, barely looking up from his scroll.

"I've come to pay for the sins of the world, Matthew."

"Do you mock..." the tax collector's head jerked up, caustic words starting to spew like hot destructive lava.

"I've come to pay for your sins, Matthew."

Gentle eyes wove an undeniable message of love and acceptance around the fibers of sin and failure within the tax collector until he nearly choked. Stumbling to his feet, scattering scrolls and coins on the ground, Matthew reached out to the man who dared to confront him. With a grip strong, sure, and cleansing, Jesus helped Matthew rise, leaving his sins among the payments and parchments.

"Follow me, Matthew. I've great things for you to do."

"Lord, please come to my house. Let me serve you."

"I'd love to have dinner with you, Matthew."

"Would you mind if some of my friends join us? I want to tell them what you've done for me," Matthew asked hesitantly.

"Of course, it's your home and your friends. I'm just a guest," Jesus smiled.

"Far from it, Lord! You looked beyond the tax collecting, the greed, all I've taken from my people. You looked beyond the sin and saw me! How can I thank you?"

Jesus grinned, and said, "Matthew, you are our heavenly Father's son, just as I am. I came so you may have life and live it abundantly. It pleases our Father that you're willing to accept and share his gift of eternal life, and that you want to share it with others. I look forward to sharing a meal with you and your friends."

About sundown, Jesus followed the directions Matthew had given him to his home. It was in a neighborhood he had not been in before with large, ornate houses attended by sour-faced servants. Matthew's house was easy to spot with lots of lights, and lots of people coming and going. A smile tugged at the corner of Jesus's mouth as he spotted a group of Pharisees going into the house.

Poor Matthew! Tax collectors and Pharisees together in one place can only mean trouble for him.

"Heavenly Father, thank you for my new brother, Matthew," Jesus prayed as he paused briefly in front of the house. "Thank you for the lives he will touch, and the work he will accomplish for your kingdom. I thank you for his zeal to share his newfound hope and purpose with his peers.

"I pray you'll be with him tonight as his faith faces its first challenges. Help his heart, mind, and spirit hold tight to the vision you have granted him. Give him your peace within to withstand attacks. Thank you for loving both Matthew and me. In your holy name, amen."

Finishing his prayer as he approached the gate to the house, Jesus threw back his shoulders and clasped his chest as if he was putting on a breastplate. He looked like a veteran soldier, ready for combat.

"Lord, you've come! I was afraid you'd change your mind," Matthew loudly greeted him.

"I've never broken a promise, Matthew," he replied with compassion and authority. "Introduce me to your friends. I asked a couple of mine to join me here as well."

Groups of visitors seemed to part before them like wheat in the wind. The two men stopped occasionally and chatted congenially with guests, taking their time to move about the crowded house. Observers noticed Matthew's new friend seemed to smile a little, as if thinking of a private joke.

Soon the feast was brought to the tables. Matthew offered the best place to his new friend, while other tax collectors jockeyed for seats near the head of the table. The Pharisees and scribes tried to blend in with other guests so they could watch, and listen to, interactions among the diverse guests seated at the table.

The man some were beginning to call the Messiah was seated at the right hand of Matthew, who had been known for cheating his own people with surplus taxes. One guest could be overheard saying that was how Matthew paid for this lavish home, with its many servants and bountiful feast. Some of the so-called Messiah's followers were with him, mingling with Matthew's pitiful band of moneymakers.

"How dare he proclaim himself to be the Son of God and sit down to eat with such sinners!" said one of the Pharisees disgustedly.

"A traveler from Galilee said he had the nerve to stand up and preach in their synagogue like he had a right to," responded the scribe next to him, shaking his head in amazement.

"Here comes one of his followers now. Hey, Galilean! Why does your friend lower himself to eat with sinners and tax collectors? Isn't he afraid it will hurt his reputation?" Disdain dripped from the temple leader's words, as pomegranate juice dripped from his beard.

Before the last syllable could leave the Pharisee's lips, Jesus stood up painstakingly slow from the table and walked toward the Pharisee. In a voice that resonated power and accusation, he said to him, "If you question my actions or motives, why ask my disciples? *Ask me yourself!*"

"We're only trying to understand why someone who calls himself the Son of God and acts like a rabbi is sitting at the table with sinners," the Pharisee snarled, standing up and jutting out his chin.

"I could ask you, the most pious, the most righteous men of the city the same question," Jesus said in a low voice, his upper lip curling. "Are you truly sons of God? You wonder why the Son of God would fellowship with sinners? Do you also wonder why the sick and lame would seek a physician?" Jesus parried.

"Of course not! But that doesn't explain why you're eating in the house of a...a tax collector," sneered the Pharisee.

"Perhaps you should search Scripture to understand, 'I desire mercy, not sacrifice.' I came to seek and love those who don't quite measure up, not the uptight, upright, not the seemingly righteous like you," Jesus answered him, his back ramrod straight and eyes hardening with the last word.

While Jesus and the Pharisee bantered back and forth, Matthew made his way to them through the crowded room. He touched Jesus on the shoulder as the Pharisees stalked angrily away.

"Is everything all right, Lord? I would hate for someone to ruin our celebration. My friends are saying they want to ask you more questions. Do you mind?"

"Everything is fine, Matthew. It's a wonderful party, and I would love to talk with your friends," he beamed at Matthew.

The two men walked back to their places at the table, Jesus's arm tossed over Matthew's shoulder, and the two of them chuckling like old friends.

BIBLE REFERENCE: Matthew 9:9–13 *The Message*

9 Passing along, Jesus saw a man at his work collecting taxes. His name was Matthew. Jesus said, "Come along with me." Matthew stood up and followed him.

10–11 Later when Jesus was eating supper at Matthew's house with his close followers, a lot of disreputable characters came and joined them. When the Pharisees saw him keeping this kind of company, they had a fit, and lit into Jesus' followers. "What kind of example is this from your Teacher, acting cozy with crooks and riffraff?"

12–13 Jesus, overhearing, shot back, "Who needs a doctor: the healthy or the sick? Go figure out what this Scripture means: 'I'm after mercy, not religion.' I'm here to invite outsiders, not coddle insiders."

*How do you handle bullies?
Do you find it easier to stick up
for yourself or others?*

Calm in the Storm

The day had been long. Crowds of needy people kept growing, kept coming. Not only was Jesus weary, he could tell by his disciples' hunched shoulders and dull eyes that they were too.

The disciples never ceased to amaze him. They weren't perfect by any means, but by and large they brought the same servant hearts and devotion they had for their families to the crowds who came seeking Jesus and the love he preached about. Jesus couldn't imagine doing the work his Father had given him without these men.

Judas, on the other hand, seemed only concerned about the business end of the ministry. Sadly, Judas had not come to the same realization as Matthew that some things are far more valuable than mere coins.

These men. These diverse, and sometimes challenging, men. These men who had left everything familiar to follow him. These men whom he loved now needed a break from serving others.

"Peter, James, John, round up the others and let's go to the other side of the lake," Jesus called to his companions.

"Jesus, the men are tired. Couldn't we rest here a bit?" questioned James.

"How can we rest when the needy never seem to stop coming for Jesus's touch?" Peter jumped in.

"Come, we'll go to the other side where it is calmer and quieter," said Jesus.

"Jesus, it looks like a storm is brewing. Do you really think it's a good idea to go out on the lake?" Thomas seemed to question and hesitate far more than the others.

"It will be fine. Let's get into the boats." Jesus's tone resonated with authority as he started toward the boats, expecting the men to follow without any further discussion.

Seeing the men move toward the boats, dragging their feet, those coming to be healed and helped were visibly deflated by piercing disappointment. Jesus looked at them with compassion, knowing their needs would not diminish, and that he would return to them soon. Right now, he needed to tend to his inner circle. Rest was a rare commodity for all of them.

"John, are you ready to shove off?" Andrew shouted across the waves to the other boat. Andrew didn't envy John having Thomas in his boat. Thomas and Judas were hunkering down in the back of the fishing boat, not looking at all pleased about their departure.

"We're ready when you are," John called over the rising winds.

While the sailors made the boats ready, Jesus found a spot near the back of one. The leather cushions in the boat were as welcome as couches of down and silk for bodies used to sitting and sleeping on hard ground. Jesus was already settling in and looking drowsy when ropes were untethered and tossed into the bottoms of the boats.

The pairs of fishing brothers were used to being the only specks of light caught between dark skies and black seas. With fishing the only source of income for their families, the men were also accustomed to being on the water in all kinds of weather. Jesus dozed off in the back of Peter and Andrew's boat, fully confident in their skill on the lake. He wasn't worried at all about the darkening skies. His confidence in the fishermen spread a blanket of peace over the other passengers.

The fishermen sometimes joked about being born with oars in their hands. The surety of long experience showed in their work. Few words between the sailors were needed as they steered their boats, using only a look, nod, or simple gesture to communicate.

After a particularly long day of ministering to the sick, the sad, and the downtrodden, the fishermen sometimes talked longingly of the less taxing days of "just" fishing. They were glad to be able to man rudders and sails on occasion, finding their tugs and pulls less strenuous than the tugging and pulling of the disabled and the disenfranchised.

The shore faded behind them as the boats slipped through the sea. Muscles taut, eyes focused, the navigators were the first ones to notice a disturbance moving quickly toward the boats. Before they could caution their passengers to secure themselves and their bundles, great waves rose up to engulf the boats. Unrelenting whitecaps slammed against the sides, leaving no time to catch a breath between assaults.

Passengers and sailors grabbed at oars, sails, anything to gain balance. Instructions, encouragement, all words were ripped from their lips. Peter, who had seemed to be such a bulwark upon the sea, now stumbled and flailed about as he tried to reach Jesus. Nearly blinded by the rain, Peter strained to keep a grip on anything while moving towards the back of the boat.

"Master! Master!" the words tore from Peter's lungs. Jesus didn't move or shift in the boat bouncing on the waves. "Jesus? Jesus! Can you hear me?" Peter's agonizing, desperate words were a whisper in the gales.

Jesus slowly shrugged and sat up, rubbing his eyes and shaking his hair. His face unmarked by concern about the tempest threatening them.

"Master, please do something! We're about to perish!"

"Peter, do you think I brought all of you out here to die?" Jesus said, chastisement in his voice.

"Lord, we're sinking! Save us!"

Clutching ropes, masts, whatever they could reach, the terrified men looked to their leader for any hope. Astonishingly sure-footed, Jesus rose confidently in the reeling boat.

"Peace! Be still!" his voice rang out over the winds and waves, his face full of power and radiance.

The air surrounding the tossing boats seemed to take a breath, then softly exhale. Just as quickly as it arose, the storm dissolved, leaving only drenched, exhausted and astonished men in its wake.

Shaking his head and dragging a hand through his dripping hair, Jesus looked sternly at the bewildered faces of his disciples.

"I call you disciples, followers, my inner circle, for crying out loud! How could you be so faithless, so flat-out terrified?

I can't believe you still don't completely trust me after all this time, after all you've seen and we've done."

Weak words dribbled from mouths full of excuses. Their lack of understanding must be as foreign to him as his power was to them. Like the waves that melted into the gentle rhythm of the sea, excuses dissolved and heads hung low.

"You marvel and wonder that the winds and the seas obey me, and yet you have witnessed many other miracles at my hand. Have I not told you, do you still not believe that I am the Son of God? My power and works aren't of this world!"

Seeing confusion and disappointment in their slumping shoulders, Jesus switched gears and began talking to the disciples tenderly, as their heavenly Father would to his frightened children.

"I've called some of you "sons of thunder" and certainly you are. You have weathered many storms of life. You'll also weather storms of faith, but you don't have to be afraid. Just as I'm with you now, I will be with you everywhere and always."

One by one faces lifted, smiles began to overcome worried brows. Jesus looked at each one, touched a hand, a face, a shoulder, reassuring, loving each one. Slowly, the curtain of fright and frailty was torn in two, replaced by hope and confidence. Seeing one transformation after another, joy and laughter gained footholds in Jesus until he could contain it no longer, and laughter spilled out of him.

"Each of you has been called with a plan and a purpose, and it's not perishing in the sea today. You're amazed at the calming of the storm . . . just wait! You will also do wonders and miracles in my name. Let's celebrate that our heavenly Father has chosen to come to live with and work in us!"

Jesus's words of confidence seemed to saturate the men in the boat with hope and understanding as they journeyed calmly to the far shore. A mantle of peace settled on those who would hear, giving the men rest from the sea and the needs of the crowds.

Calloused feet in worn sandals splashed through the water as roughened hands grabbed ropes to pull the boats ashore. While the group was making their way to a clearing on the edge of the beach, Jesus's fellow passengers were as captivated listening him share the words of encouragement with their friends from the other boat as they were after he calmed the storm.

A few gathered wood and rocks for a fire; others caught fish for their supper. Taking soaked cloaks and spreading them on nearby bushes, Jesus smiled as he listened to the men's excited chatter about what they had experienced, and laughter at themselves for all they still had to learn.

Jesus wandered away from the small gathering while the fish were cleaned and placed on the fire. As much as he loved these men who answered the call to follow him, Jesus loved moments of quiet communion with his heavenly Father more. Just as the calming of the storm had filled the disciples with awe, Jesus was filled with awe by the endless love and patience the Father continued to show them.

Walking along the shore, Jesus's heart leapt with pure joy, smelling the aroma of cooking fish and hearing the sounds of his saints. His joy mingled with the fragrance and fellowship as it rose to become incense of praise for all the Father was doing, and would continue to do, in the lives of his children.

> *Think about a time when you taught someone something that seemed important. Maybe teaching a teenager to balance a checkbook, or a new person in the next cubicle how the office software works. Was it smooth sailing the whole way, or was a little head banging involved? Think about what it was like from the perspectives of both teacher and pupil.*

BIBLE REFERENCE: Mark 4:35–41 The Message

35–38 Late that day he said to them, "Let's go across to the other side." They took him in the boat as he was. Other boats came along. A huge storm came up. Waves poured into the boat, threatening to sink it. And Jesus was in the stern, head on a pillow, sleeping! They roused him, saying, "Teacher, is it nothing to you that we're going down?"

39–40 Awake now, he told the wind to pipe down and said to the sea, "Quiet! Settle down!" The wind ran out of breath; the sea became smooth as glass. Jesus reprimanded the disciples: "Why are you such cowards? Don't you have any faith at all?"

41 They were in absolute awe, staggered. "Who is this, anyway?" they asked. "Wind and sea at his beck and call!"

Mob Mentality

The men who had staggered onto the beach were still sopping wet and silent. They were wrung out physically and mentally from fighting the violent storm on the lake, from trying to make sense of a teacher who could calm it with his words. Returning to the crowds the next day had been fulfilling in its service, but tiring with another trip upon the lake.

Jesus walked purposefully ahead of his followers, shaking his head as he recalled their continued amazement and unbelief. When would this motley crew he called his disciples figure out that he really was who he said he was?

The teacher and his followers were jerked from their thoughts by a naked man running right at them and screaming bloody murder. This guy was overrun with issues, no doubt about it. Aside from the whole nudity thing, the men could easily see scratches and bruises all over the man, and what looked like shackles on one of his hands.

"Jesus! Jesus! I know who you are!" a voice filled with gravel and the groaning of a wild beast grumbled. Collapsing right in the middle of the road in front of Jesus, the man growled, "I know you are the Son of God; did you come to torment me?"

Focusing solely on the one at his feet, Jesus knelt by the man, and gently lifted his chin. Looking into eyes brimming with terror, tears, and pain, he asked, "What's your name?"

In little more than a whisper, he whimpered, "Mob . . . sometimes they call me Legion. You're right to call me out. I am too many to continue in this pitiful frame, but don't send me into a bottomless pit." The man struggled to sit up, then looked around and pointed. "You see that bunch of pigs, Son of God? Cast me into them instead."

Placing both hands on the man's head, Jesus commanded the demons to come out of him and into the pigs. The pigs immediately went berserk. They stampeded over a precipice into the lake and drowned.

The disciples were standing there with their mouths hanging open, and so were the pig herders, but only for a minute. The herders snapped out of their astonishment at what this man, Jesus, had just done to their pigs. In just a few seconds, they flipped the script from amazement to rage then dashed into town to tell everyone about the atrocity that had happened.

"John, would you and the guys round up some food and clothing for our new friend," Jesus said, never taking his eyes from the man's. Jesus sat cross-legged on the ground with the man leaning against him, breathing easily, muscles relaxed. Jesus stroked his head as a parent would a child. "I think I'll call you Genesis," Jesus said to him. "*Mob* doesn't seem to suit you now."

"A new beginning, that's what you've given me," the man smiled. "I like it! A new name to go with a new life."

John and the other men rummaged through their bundles to find spare clothes for the man to put on, and for a bit of bread and cheese. Some of the disciples hung back from approaching Jesus and the man, rechristened as "Genesis."

Seeing them hesitate, Peter grabbed a spare tunic and cloak from them, "What are you guys afraid of? This is still Jesus! If Jesus can cast the demons out of this man, the least we can do is to share a couple of garments and food." Peter shook his head, then turned on his heel and went to where Jesus and Genesis were sitting and talking quietly.

Soon after, Genesis, now fully clothed, was finishing the bread and cheese when the pig herders and townspeople barreled into the clearing with shouts and clubs. At first, they didn't recognize the man they knew as Mob, crazy and frequently violent. Puzzled, they stopped in their tracks and looked closer at the small group.

"Hey, you're Mob! You're the guy who used to run around the cemetery naked!" one man called and pointed.

Genesis glanced at Jesus, who nodded slightly, then said, "Yes, I was. Now I'm a new man. My name is Genesis because Jesus has given me a new beginning, a new life."

More than one mouth fell open to see and hear any kind of sense coming from someone who had lived a despicable life until that day. The herders and townspeople let their clubs and makeshift weapons drop to their sides. Some of them fell to their knees, seeing the impossible made possible. Soon, whispers began to float among the group.

"Who is this man, Jesus?"

"What are his men up to? Can they do all he does?"

"What's he going to do next?"

As the voices got louder, the disciples gathered their belongings and made their way to where Jesus continued to sit. They were ready for his instructions.

One of the pig herders stepped to the front of the locals. "Who do you think you are to come into our community and begin messing with people?"

"Everything was just fine until you showed up!" another herder called out. "How are we going to support our families with no pigs?"

Whispers accelerated into grumbling, then shouting and fist shaking.

Jesus stood as his disciples circled around behind him. The line between the two groups was clearly drawn. "Which is greater, for this man to be healed and restored to you, or for his demons to have destroyed your herd?"

The grumbling intensified to shouts of fear and anger.

"Jesus, let me go with you, please! I can't stay with these people any longer," the man begged, standing and pulling at Jesus's arm.

"That's right, Jesus, this is no place for your crowd or for Mob, even if he did change his name and put on clothes! All of you, hit the road or the boats, and get out of here!" The head pig herder yelled, taking a few menacing steps toward Jesus, the disciples, and Genesis.

Putting his arm around the man's shoulder, and grasping his hand, Jesus said quietly to Genesis," My work here is finished. **I came for you,**" he smiled into the man's eyes. "Your work is just beginning. I need you to visit the villages around here and tell them what I did for you. Can you do that for me?"

Genesis leaned into Jesus and dropped his head on his savior's shoulder. Jesus whispered something in his ear, then patted him on the back.

Slowly, Genesis straightened his shoulders, lifted his chin, and tried to smile at Jesus. He headed toward the road to the next village, plodding at first. A quick glance back and a wave at Jesus. Then Genesis shook himself as if waking from sleep, turned and began his new journey with long, confident strides.

The "mob" of pig herders and townspeople's grumblings grew louder as they shook their fists and clubs at Jesus and his disciples.

"Well, guys, it looks like it's time to go! Thanks for helping out with our new friend," Jesus said, clapping one disciple then another on the back. "Andrew, James, are the boats ready to go?"

The angry mob, who only a moment ago had nearly worked themselves into a riotous frenzy, separated like waves sliced by the bow of a boat as Jesus and his band of disciples passed through to the lake's edge. It had been an exhausting day for all of them. Hopefully, it would be a peaceful journey to their next stop, but the disciples had learned that Jesus never seemed to run out of surprises.

BIBLE REFERENCE: Luke 8:26–39 The Message

26–29 They sailed on to the country of the Gerasenes, directly opposite Galilee. As he stepped out onto land, a madman from town met him; he was a victim of demons. He hadn't worn clothes for a long time, nor lived at home; he lived in the cemetery. When he saw Jesus he screamed, fell before him, and bellowed, "What business do you have messing with me? You're Jesus, Son of the High God, but don't give me a hard time!" (The man said this because Jesus had started to order the unclean spirit out of him.) Time after time the demon threw the man into convulsions. He had been placed under constant guard and tied with chains and shackles, but crazed and driven wild by the demon, he would shatter the bonds.

30–31 Jesus asked him, "What is your name?"

"Mob. My name is Mob," he said, because many demons afflicted him. And they begged Jesus desperately not to order them to the bottomless pit.

32–33 A large herd of pigs was browsing and rooting on a nearby hill. The demons begged Jesus to order them into the pigs. He gave the order. It was even worse for the pigs than for the man. Crazed, they stampeded over a cliff into the lake and drowned.

34–36 Those tending the pigs, scared to death, bolted and told their story in town and country. People went out to see what had happened. They came to Jesus and found the man from whom the demons had been sent, sitting there at Jesus' feet, wearing decent clothes and making sense. It was a holy moment, and for a short time they were more reverent than curious. Then those who had seen it happen told how the demoniac had been saved.

37–39 Later, a great many people from the Gerasene countryside got together and asked Jesus to leave—too much change, too fast, and they were scared. So Jesus got back in the boat and set off. The man whom he had delivered from the demons asked to go with him, but he sent him back, saying, "Go home and tell everything God did in you." So he went back and preached all over town everything Jesus had done in him.

> *Have you, or someone close to you, experienced a life-changing healing? Perhaps it was deliverance from cancer, or substance abuse. Maybe something seemingly smaller like lying or being judgmental. How others responded to the healing?*
>
>

You Can't Go Home Again

"Guys, what would you think about taking a couple of days off?" Jesus asked his troupe of followers as they walked along another dusty road. "I know we get pretty jazzed up when we witness spectacular healings like Peter's mother-in-law or Genesis…"

"But Jesus, I gotta tell you, they also wring me out like a dishrag," Nathanael jumped in.

"Us, too, Jesus! John and I were just talking about it. It's so amazing in the moment, but, whoa, Nelly, afterwards it's like we've been fishing for nights on end," James added.

"OK, I get the point. We could all use a little break. I was thinking we could go to Nazareth; I haven't seen my mother for a while," Jesus said.

"Since we already know she's a good cook, we're all probably good to go. Right, men?" Peter chimed in.

The group of men headed for Nazareth, talking about their families, the healings they had recently seen, and the latest news about the Roman occupation. For most of the journey Jesus seemed to have other things on his mind. Every so often one or two of the disciples would try to pull him into their conversation, but eventually they left him to his thoughts.

"Jesus, about how much longer until we get to Nazareth?" John asked. "Should we stop to eat the food we have left or muscle through?"

Jesus shook his head and looked at John as though he was just waking up. John, he thought, always looking out for others. "We'll be there just before sundown. My brothers and sisters are in and out of my mother's house all the time, so she usually fixes meals for a crowd. We can eat there this evening."

The sight of thirteen men coming into Nazareth was uncommon. Children ran to tell parents who immediately stuck their heads out of houses and shops. Many waved and called out as soon as they recognized Jesus. It was no surprise Mary was waiting at the door when Jesus and his men arrived.

This was a different side of Jesus. Usually everyone the group encountered was asking something of him, but not this time. Pure, unadulterated love lit Mary's face as she wrapped her arms around her firstborn; his face reflecting his devotion to her. The disciples stepped back to give them a little privacy for such an intimate moment.

The next few days were filled with good food, good conversation, and time to take care of mundane tasks like repairing sandals and washing whatever garments they could (or at least handing them off to Jesus's sisters to wash). Andrew and Philip wanted to replenish their food stores, but it was always like pulling teeth to get any money from Judas. Weird thing was the more relaxed the disciples became, the more restless Jesus seemed to be, constantly pacing or walking around the village.

One morning the visitors were awakened earlier than usual by the sights and smells of major cooking and cleaning.

Two of the sisters and one sister-in-law were on hand to help Mary. Jesus laughed out loud as Mary shooed him and his followers out the door.

"Mom, have we abused your hospitality by turning your house into a pigpen?"

"This may be our last Sabbath together for a while, so I want everything to be just right. Now, you and your friends go find something to do today, but be back in time to clean up for the evening meal."

As directed, Jesus and his disciples made themselves scarce, and returned to get ready for the special meal. Mary and her trio of helpers had outdone themselves. The fellowship was warm and genuine, lasting well into the night. As soon as the family members who lived elsewhere left, Mary, Jesus, and the men bedded down for the night. Well before sunrise quiet voices and feet could be heard moving about the house. Then one person left.

At the appointed time, twelve visitors arrived at the synagogue, all looking around for Jesus. They were not surprised to see him at the front, standing with the rabbis. Some of the women were still finding seats in the gallery after the men had already settled in the assembly hall. The synagogue was crowded so the disciples had to scatter themselves in order to stay in the first few rows.

All talking stopped when Jesus approached the podium and began to teach. The congregation was startled and amazed at the wisdom with which he spoke. They recalled accounts of the miracles Jesus had been doing in and around Galilee. The people marveled at the words and deeds of one who had grown up among them.

Suddenly, a man near the back stood up and shouted, "Is Jesus really all that? After all, he grew up here; his mother and sisters still live here. We know his brothers, for crying out loud."

A man closer to the front jumped up and called out, "This is Mary's son. What makes him think he's any better than the rest of us?"

Mumbling like low thunder rippled through the assembly hall. Twelve pairs of eyes looked around in astonishment. How could the wonder of the hometown crowd turn so quickly to disgust? Their eyes eventually traveled back to Jesus who had stepped from behind the podium to face the people.

"Of course, I'm Mary's son, and brother to James, Joseph, and Simon. I never denied that. But you have disdained both me and the prophecy given through me for your benefit. I should not be surprised since a prophet's hometown is usually the last place on earth he will receive the respect he deserves as God's messenger."

Once again, the assembly grew quiet. Jesus looked once more around the room at the people he had known, but saw only their rejection as some even turned their backs on him. The slaps of Jesus's sandals on the stone floor were the only sounds as he marched out of the synagogue.

The disciples were hemmed in by the angered and disgusted crowd. They couldn't get to their teacher, no matter how hard they pushed or how politely they tried to excuse themselves. The last they saw of Jesus for two days was his back, straight as a board, and his head seeming to shake in disbelief at what had just transpired.

BIBLE REFERENCE: Mark 6:1–6 Good New Translation

Soon afterwards he left that section of the country and returned with his disciples to Nazareth, his hometown. **2–3** The next Sabbath he went to the synagogue to teach, and the people were astonished at his wisdom and his miracles because he was just a local man like themselves.

"He's no better than we are," they said. "He's just a carpenter, Mary's boy, and a brother of James and Joseph, Judas and Simon. And his sisters live right here among us." And they were offended!

4 Then Jesus told them, "A prophet is honored everywhere except in his hometown and among his relatives and by his own family." **5** And because of their unbelief he couldn't do any mighty miracles among them except to place his hands on a few sick people and heal them. **6** And he could hardly accept the fact that they wouldn't believe in him. Then he went out among the villages, teaching.

---

*When was the last time
you were rejected for any reason?
How did you react?*

It's Time for Lunch!

It was a diverse group of men. Fishermen, a tax collector, a political activist, and a newer guy said to be of noble birth. And here they were, following after this guy, Jesus. Some of them weren't even sure why they'd tagged along when Jesus told, not asked, them to follow him.

The group of followers were still getting to know each other's stories in between the teaching, preaching, and healing. They'd had a little time to do that at the bash Matthew threw for Jesus at his house when he came on board. Then the Pharisees had to get all up in their business. No problemo! Jesus shut them down in the blink of an eye. And the few days staying with Mary in Jesus's hometown of Nazareth gave them a little respite before the whole ugly episode in the synagogue.

The teacher and his followers seemed to be constantly on the road. And the disciples were usually clueless about exactly where they were headed. Today the men were really puzzled since it was the Sabbath, and traveling was strictly forbidden by Jewish law. The weird thing was Jesus didn't seem overly concerned about sticking to all the rules and regulations like the priests and members of the Sanhedrin, the Jewish high court.

"Andrew," asked Philip in a hushed voice, looking around at the other disciples, "did Jesus tell you where we were going?"

Andrew stopped in his tracks and turned to look at Philip, "Why would you think that?"

"Cause you and Peter have known Jesus the longest," Philip mumbled, looking down at his feet.

"It's okay, neighbor," Andrew said, throwing his arm around Philip's shoulders. "Trust me, at this point in the game, we know what you know: Jesus has done some amazing things, he's got some good stuff to say, and he's not afraid to stand up to anybody. I could be wrong, Phil, but I think this is just the start of what's going to be a wild ride!"

The two men laughed, then talked of their hometown and families.

A cloudless sky lacked any promise of shade on the road as the sun approached midday. The company of followers was surprised when Jesus decided to cut through a wheat field instead of sticking to the road.

"Is it just me," Peter called out, "or is anybody else getting hungry?"

Walking alongside Peter, John elbowed him in the stomach and said, "You're always hungry, Peter!"

"Very funny, John!"

"This grain looks pretty ripe to me, men," Jesus said, running a hand through stalks of wheat.

"Looks like a pretty good snack to me!" Peter said, grabbing a handful of heads from the grain, and beginning to rub the husks off.

"Peter! For crying out loud: we don't know whom this field belongs to. They may not like us helping ourselves," Andrew chided his brother just as Peter popped the kernels of wheat into his mouth.

"It's okay, Andrew," Jesus said. "You see those men over there on the edge of the field, I'll bet they can tell us who this field belongs to. And I'm sure Judas won't mind paying the owner for our snack to tide us over, will you, Judas?" Jesus smiled at the self-appointed CFO of the group.

"Humph!" Judas spewed, sending a withering look toward their leader.

Tossing a couple of kernels in his mouth, Matthew said, "These aren't too bad, Peter. Judas, you should try a few, and if you need any help figuring out how much to pay the landowner, let me know."

Muffled laughter ran through the men as all but Judas began sampling the grain.

"Hey, Jesus, did you know the Pharisees had a welcome committee for us?" asked John.

"Pipe down, John," James hissed. "These guys look fit to be tied and that probably means trouble for us."

Without breaking his stride, Jesus left the wheat field and walked to the Pharisees who stood nearby glaring at them.

One of the Pharisees puffed out his chest and waved vigorously toward the grain field, "Are you crazy? I can see you're a Jew, so I'm sure you know it's against the law to do work of any kind, including traveling or harvesting wheat, on the Sabbath."

Jesus calmly brushed the dust of the wheat from his hands and robe before looking at the trio of "Commandment Cops."

The one in the middle grew red in the face and busted out with, "Haven't you read the Scriptures? What you and your hooligans are doing is unlawful!"

"As a matter of fact, I have read the Scriptures," Jesus said, straightening his back and lifting his chin ever so slightly. "Haven't you read the part about King David feeding his soldiers with the bread made only for the priests to eat? While you were at it, did you read that the temple guards who are 'working,' doing their assigned duties, on the Sabbath aren't breaking the law?"

The Pharisees tugged on their beards even as their eyes seemed to bulge out of their heads in exasperation. Who did this man think he was? Didn't he realize the power they wielded?

"Who do you think you are to threaten others with God's Word? Our heavenly Father made the Sabbath for man, not the other way around. And by the way, that includes the Son of Man. And just to be clear, the Son of Man is Lord of all, including the Sabbath." Jesus dusted off his hands again. Finished with the grain, finished with this ridiculous conversation, and finished with these petty men, Jesus turned on his heel and walked away.

After chomping down on one last mouthful of wheat kernels, Andrew strode up to Philip and shoulder bumped him, "Didn't I tell you it was going to be a wild ride, Phillip?"

BIBLE REFERENCE: Luke 6:1-5 The Passion Translation

1 One Sabbath day, Jesus and his disciples were walking through a field of ripe wheat. His disciples plucked some heads of grain and rubbed the husks off with their hands and ate it. **2** This infuriated some of the Jewish religious leaders. They said to Jesus, "Why are you allowing your disciples to harvest grain on the Sabbath day? Don't you know it's not permissible according to the law?"

3 Jesus replied, "Haven't you read the Scriptures? Haven't you read what King David did when he was hungry? **4** He entered the sanctuary of God, took the bread of God's presence right off the sacred table, and shared it with his men. [a] It was only lawful for the priests to eat the bread of God's presence. **5** You need to know that the Son of Man is no slave to the Sabbath day, for I am master over the Sabbath."

There's probably never been a time without injustice. Sometimes heroes arise, and many times the world never hears of them. Describe someone in your world that stood in the gap against injustice?

The Jesus Connection

"Philip, make sure all but one of those baskets of food is sent to the poor in town. Peter, put the remaining basket in the boat for us to have later," Jesus called out over the dwindling crowd of people.

The disciples were still scratching their heads over Jesus turning a few loaves of bread and fish into a meal for everyone. Being the "math guys," Matthew and Judas estimated the men in the crowd to number around five thousand. It could be nearly double that when you added the women and kids. There was no way even the math guys could understand multiplication by Jesus. And he was never one to waste time, so Jesus was already moving on to the next item on the agenda.

"How does he do that?" Philip asked, moving baskets of leftovers to one place.

"Do what?"

"You know, Peter: first we hear Herod executed John the Baptist. Before Jesus had a minute to grieve for his cousin, this huge crowd shows up, and he unbelievably feeds all of them."

"I think Jesus has some kind of on and off switch," Peter said, hauling another basket to the ones headed for the poor. "How many times have we seen him, worn out from preaching and traveling, or disgusted with the Pharisees, but as soon as the needy show up he turns into some kind of superhero, touching, healing, telling them what they need to hear?"

"Sure, I've seen Jesus flip the script too. I just don't understand how he does it," Philip said, plopping down on the grass beside the baskets.

"Hey, Matthew, could you and Judas round up some guys to take these baskets of leftovers into the villages?" Peter hollered to his friend, then turned to Philip chuckling. "Don't you know that will aggravate the living daylights out of Judas? He hates sharing anything with anybody."

Philip laughed quietly, then asked, "Where are Andrew and James?"

"Jesus said to get ready to head back to the other side of the lake so they're probably getting the boats ready," Peter said, collapsing onto the grass near the baskets.

The men soaked up the aroma and coolness of the grass. The group of followers was nearly as tired as their leader. The food monitors had almost dozed off when a slim shadow fell across their faces.

"Thanks for getting that all together," Jesus told Philip and Peter, his words quiet and slow. "I know I can always count on you. As soon as all the baskets have been handed out, hit the boats. I'll meet you on the other side." Jesus turned and walked away like his feet were made of iron.

"Jesus!" Peter called, "How are you going to get there?" Peter's words seem to hang in the evening air as Jesus kept walking.

"Where's he going?" Judas snarled at the followers. "I've got these two guys to take food baskets to their villages for the poor." Leaning down to Peter and Philip, he dropped his voice and said, "What do you wanna bet the baskets never make it past their own front doors?"

Peter jumped to his feet, nearly knocking Judas down. "Why can't you just do what the Master tells you for once, Judas, instead of always doubting him or the outcome?"

As soon as the villagers had taken the last basket of leftovers, the disciples headed to the boats. It was a long haul across the Sea of Galilee and it was already getting dark.

"Peter, quit messing around and get into the boat," Andrew yelled to his brother over his shoulder as he hoisted the sails. "It looks like a storm may be headed our way."

"Go, ahead, bro, shove off! I'm coming and you know me, I don't mind getting my feet wet," Peter hollered back, starting to run toward the boat.

"Matthew, Judas, come on!" James waved to his friends. "At the rate you two are going Jesus is going to beat us to the other side."

Once all the disciples had boarded the boats, every man was on an oar or a sail fighting the storm that quickly overtook them. Muscles strained to keep the boats afloat. Voices grew hoarse and raspy as they yelled directions back and forth. Lightning occasionally splits the sky. Robes had been stripped off hours ago and tossed into the bottoms of the boats before the wind could rip them to shreds.

"John, did you see that?" James yelled to his brother before dawn began to awaken.

"Was it lightning?" John asked, stretching his neck and straining to see.

Glancing toward the other boat, the men saw Peter waving and pointing as the light moved toward the boats.

"I knew this was a bad idea." The shrillness of Judas's whine could be heard over the howling wind. "We're all gonna die: I just know it! Look! Over there! It's a ghost coming to bring bad omens! "

"Shut up, Judas! Jesus wouldn't let us die now," James hollered in Judas's direction.

"James, what's Peter doing? It looks like he's moving to the edge of the boat. What did he just say?"

Peter clawed his way through tangled ropes, exhausted men, and cast-off robes trying to get to the side of the boat. He cupped his eyes trying to see more clearly. The other disciples were holding on for dear life.

"Jesus! Jesus, is it you?" The wind ripped the words from Peter's lips.

"Buck up, men! It's me! No worries!" Jesus called to his men.

"Jesus! Tell me to come to you and I will!" Peter screamed, tossing off his sandals, then throwing one leg over the side of the boat.

"Come on, Peter! You can do it, just put your foot on the water," Jesus called to him, reaching out his hand.

With his eyes squarely on Jesus, Peter began to walk across the water to him. But the wind still howled and the waves still lapped over the sides of the boats. For a millisecond, Peter glanced down. That was all it took for him to be seized by the angry waves.

"Master, save me!" Peter's words were slapped about, hitting one disciple after another right between the eyes. Panic, anguish, terror gripped them. They were all captured by Peter's desperate plea.

Without flinching, Jesus's hand stretched out and connected with Peter's contorted fingers. With seemingly little effort, Jesus pulled Peter from the water and clasped him to his side. "Oh, feeble-hearted man . . . Why did you doubt me?"

As soon as the feet of Jesus and Peter touched the bottom of the boat, the wind calmed down. Mouths dropped open, eyes bugged out as the disciples looked at Jesus, then Peter, and then hit their knees.

"Friends, will you ever cease to doubt me? What will it take for you to fully understand and embrace that God is my Father? He lives and moves in me, and I in Him. This is no phony baloney magic act! You have seen the hand of God work through me with your own eyes. It's time you get a grip."

BIBLE REFERENCE: Matthew 14:22–33 The Message

22–23 As soon as the meal was finished, he insisted that the disciples get in the boat and go on ahead to the other side while he dismissed the people. With the crowd dispersed, he climbed the mountain so he could be by himself and pray. He stayed there alone, late into the night.

24–26 Meanwhile, the boat was far out to sea when the wind came up against them and they were battered by the waves. At about four o'clock in the morning, Jesus came toward them walking on the water. They were scared out of their wits. "A ghost!" they said, crying out in terror.

27 But Jesus was quick to comfort them. "Courage, it's me. Don't be afraid."

28 Peter, suddenly bold, said, "Master. If it's really you, call me to come to you on the water."

29–30 He said, "Come ahead."

Jumping out of the boat, Peter walked on the water to Jesus. But when he looked down at the waves churning beneath his feet, he lost his nerve and started to sink. He cried, "Master, save me!"

31 Jesus didn't hesitate. He reached down and grabbed his hand. Then he said, "Faint-heart, what got into you?"

32–33 The two of them climbed into the boat, and the wind died down. The disciples in the boat, having watched the whole thing, worshiped Jesus, saying, "This is it! You are God's Son for sure!"

What is the most recent thing you've witnessed that filled your heart with wonder and your mind with questions?

What Were You Thinking?

Jesus slowed his pace. Though his followers called him "Rabbi," "Teacher," sometimes even "Master," he had no synagogue to teach them in. Their classroom was under a tree, in the fields, on the road.

Time was running out and he had so much to teach them. So many people to minister to. There was no time to stop for today's pivotal lesson, but this topic must be broached. Everything depended on the disciples' complete understanding.

Stopping in the middle of the road, Jesus turned to this group of men he had grown to love and motioned them to gather around him. Slowly, the stream of men became a bottleneck hovering around their leader and headed toward their next destination.

"Brothers, I've been wondering: who do people think I am?" Jesus asked.

His followers' footsteps began to drag, to falter slightly. Was this a trick question? What was the teacher really wanting to know? Silence hung like dust in the air for a couple of minutes as the men continued their journey.

"I've heard some people say you're John the Baptist, Rabbi," offered Andrew.

"Me too, but some people also think you're the prophet, Elijah, risen from the dead," Philip said.

"A lot of people are just looking for someone to heal them, but a few have said they think you're one of the prophets of old," John added.

"Okay, that's all good to know," Jesus said, then stopped and turned to face the group. "What I really want to know is who *you* think I am?"

Before another step could be taken, Peter spoke up, "Jesus, you're the Son of God!"

A few gasps escaped the followers, then more silence. Jesus took a minute to look closely into each man's eyes. "For now, let's just keep this to ourselves," he said, reaching out to touch a shoulder, a hand to relieve the astonishment he saw in the faces around him.

As the somber band of disciples headed down the road, Jesus began to fill them in on what they could expect in the short and long hauls.

"Things are going to get pretty ugly very soon. I don't want you to be surprised by what is going to happen. The head honchos are going to turn on me in a major way. There's going to be a kangaroo court, some nasty interrogations, and I'll be executed. But, listen up, this is the biggie: after three days, our Heavenly Father will raise me from the dead!"

Of one accord, the teacher and disciples once again paused in the road. Jesus gave them a moment to let what he had just shared sink in.

A strong hand tugging on his arm turned Jesus around from looking at his followers. "Jesus! Jesus, what are you thinking?"

Peter hissed. "You can't be saying stuff like that! We're in and out of trouble enough as it is."

One look from Jesus and Peter immediately let go of his arm and stepped back. Peter hadn't seen so much anger in Jesus's eyes since he tossed the tables in the temple.

"Back off, Satan! You only try to tempt me away from my Father's will!"

Heads reeled. Mouths gaped. Eyes nearly spun in their sockets. What had just happened? The sun suddenly seemed hotter. Pebbles in sandals felt like boulders. Bedrolls and skins of water doubled in weight. Jesus had done an abrupt about-face. Everything around them felt heavy.

Jesus shook himself and looked upward. The band of erstwhile believers stood staring at anything but each other or him. Then he shrugged and began putting one foot in front of the other.

One by one the disciples began walking after Jesus.

As the men neared the first village in Caesarea Philippi, locals began to join them. New voices began to mingle with those of the disciples. Still in the throes of confusion from Jesus's brusque change of attitude, at first the men hesitantly answered their questions about the man, Jesus, his healing, but deflected any about his theology.

A small hill with a few trees edged the last bend in the road just as village houses came into view. Jesus took the slight incline in stride, climbing to the shade of the tallest tree and having a seat.

"Come, children, we have things to talk about," Jesus called, then leaned against the tree. For a moment he closed his eyes while the growing crowd gathered about him.

Out of habit or obedience, twelve men formed a semi-circle flanking Jesus. Judas Iscariot sat in his usual place furthest from Jesus. He looked up from counting coins in the group's moneybag, surprised to see Peter sitting down beside him.

Jesus took his time looking around at the faces of his followers, and then the townsfolk before him. Each one had a story. Stories of longing, joy, disappointment, pain. He looked away for a second and breathed a prayer.

"Father, the ones you have chosen to walk with me especially need to know what I am about to tell them. Help me get it right, to tell them in a way they will understand and embrace."

"Dear Ones, you follow me up a hill to a shady place. Very soon you'll have to make a decision whether or not to follow me any further. The path I'm taking will be hard; sometimes it will seem unbearable. But, children, the good news is that God has a plan for each of your lives. You're lost if you try to work out all the details of your own life.

"It's only in totally submitting yourselves to his plans that you'll find your lives. Part of God's plan for you is to let others know he wants to be a major player in your lives and theirs. If you're too embarrassed to share that, then I'll be embarrassed to tell our heavenly Father I know you. This is a big deal, people. Please don't miss it! Come and follow me, not for my sake, but for yours."

A slight breeze churned the branches on the trees, bringing respite from the heat. Jesus leaned his head against the tree and closed his eyes for a heartbeat. The whisper of the breeze sounded like a benediction to the challenge he had put before the small congregation of followers and seekers. In the distance a mother's voice called her children into supper.

"My friends," Jesus said, rising from his seat upon the ground, "apparently it's time to eat!"

Hungry children jumped up and began pulling their mothers' hands. Jesus smiled and nodded a dismissal to them. Some of the men hung back, making their ways to the disciples and Jesus.

Just as the sun began to set, the last villager grudgingly made his way home. Jesus watched them go as a father watches his children leave his home for the last time.

"Master?" a low voice rumbled.

"Peter!" Jesus yelled, then fiercely grabbed him in a bear hug. Finally pulling back so he could see Peter's face, Jesus said, "Peter, it's going to be a hard road ahead. I've spoken to all of you from what I know, not just what I think. Do you hear me, Peter, really hear me? It's going to be tough and those who choose to follow me must know that now or they will fall away. I haven't said these things out of a place of arrogance or intimidation, but of love. Does it make a little more sense now?"

"It's a lot to take in, Jesus," Peter said. Throwing his shoulders back, he looked Jesus right in the eye. "It's a lot, but I still choose to follow you."

"Good man, Peter!" Jesus chuckled. "Now, let's go see about some supper," he said, throwing an arm around the fisherman's shoulder.

BIBLE REFERENCE: Mark 8:27–38 The Voice

27 As He traveled with His disciples into the villages of Caesarea Philippi, He posed an *important* question to them.

Jesus: Who do the people say that I am?

28 They told Him *about the great speculation concerning His identity.*

Disciples: Some of them say *You are* John the Baptist, [a] others say Elijah, while others say one of the prophets *of old.*

Jesus *(pressing the question)*: **29** And who do you say that I am?

Peter: You are God's Anointed, *the Liberating King.*

Jesus: 30 Don't tell anyone. *It is not yet time.*

31 And He went on to teach them many things *about Himself:* how the Son of Man would suffer; how He would be rejected by the elders, chief priests, and scribes; how He would be killed; and how, after three days, *God would raise Him* from the dead.

32 He said all these things in front of them all, but Peter took Jesus aside to rebuke Him.

(Peter represents the best and worst in humanity. One day, Peter drops everything to become a follower of Jesus; the next, he's busy putting his foot in his mouth. Peter is always responding to Jesus, frequently making mistakes, but never drifting far from Jesus' side. In this passage, Peter verbalizes God's word and Satan's temptation—almost in the same breath. Peter thinks he understands who Jesus is, but he still has a lot to learn about what Jesus has come to do.)

Jesus *(seeing His disciples surrounding them)*: **33** Get behind Me, you tempter! You're thinking only of human things, not of the things God has planned.

34 He gathered the crowd and His disciples alike.

Jesus: If any one of you wants to follow Me, you'll have to give yourself up to God's plan, take up your cross, and do as I do. **35** For any one of you who wants to be rescued will lose your life, but any one of you who loses your life for My sake and for the sake of this good news will be liberated. **36** Really, what profit is there for you to gain the whole world and lose yourself *in the process*? **37** What can you give in exchange for your life? **38** If you are ashamed of Me and of what I came to teach to this adulterous and sinful generation, then the Son of Man will be ashamed of you when He comes in the glory of His Father along with the holy messengers *at the final judgment.*

> *Has there been a time you had a sense of urgency about something you wanted to share with another person? Perhaps a job promotion, a new boyfriend or girlfriend. Maybe there's going to be a downsize at work or one less place at your table. How did you frame the conversation?*

Extravagant Love

"Jesus, are you sure this is a good idea? If the Pharisees wouldn't listen to John the Baptist, why do you think they'll listen to you?" Peter said, leaning toward Jesus.

"Yeah, Jesus. What if they're just setting you up? Those guys are powerful; they can put us in prison based on their word against ours," Matthew cautioned.

As if on command, thirteen men stopped in the road, twelve pairs of eyes focused on only one of them.

"Peter, Matthew, all of you, if I can heal the sick, including an army officer's servant, for crying out loud, and raise the widow's son from the dead, don't you think I can handle a few Pharisees? I appreciate your concern, really, I do. But there's nothing to worry about."

A hand touched the teacher's sleeve. "Rabbi, maybe a couple of us should..."

"Andrew, truly, I've got this. I don't need an escort," Jesus said, turning to look at each man. "You've all been working hard. Have a good meal, relax. I'll be fine and will see you in the morning."

As they watched Jesus walk away, some of the men shook their heads and stroked their beards with worry. Others headed for the inn to get some supper.

A few blocks away, Jesus was welcomed into the lavish home of Simon the Pharisee.

"Jesus, it's so good of you to join us. Make yourself at home. We'll be eating shortly," Simon told his guest, waving his hand toward tables loaded with rich, exotic foods, and surrounded by couches covered with expensive silk and velvet throws.

Jesus made his way toward the end of one of the tables and sat down. He was just getting comfortable when he began to hear gasps and saw other guests pointing at the door. Someone had entered. Simon's guests began to plaster themselves against the walls, creating a wide pathway for the woman.

"They say she's the busiest prostitute in the city," a voice next to Jesus hissed. "I wonder what she's doing here. I can't imagine Simon inviting her. Just look how she walks. Even carrying that big jar, she looks like a walking invitation."

Jesus's eyes followed the woman around the room. When she stopped at his table, the guests around him quickly moved away. He didn't flinch, even when she knelt at his feet and opened the jar of fragrant perfume. The sweetness of the perfume filled the crowded room, mingling with the hum of gossip.

A sob ripped from the woman's throat, followed by hot tears. She kissed his tired and weary feet, letting her tears wet them. She slowly unbound her hair and let it cascade over his feet until she covered them, gently massaging her tears and the perfume she had carried into his skin.

From the corner of his eye, Jesus saw Simon approach. He glanced up to see a face filled with disgust.

"Jesus, how could you…"

"Simon, thank you for your invitation, but you have not made me feel nearly as welcome as this woman," Jesus said to his host, returning his gaze to the woman. "You didn't offer water to wash my dusty feet, while she's bathed them with her tears. A proper host would have given me a proper kiss in greeting, which you didn't, while she knelt to kiss my feet. Simon, you didn't even have a servant bring oil to anoint my head or feet. Look! You know that perfume must have cost her dearly."

"But, Jesus, she's a pros-..."

"A sinner, Simon? My heavenly Father sent me to seek and save sinners, to lift them up, not grind them under my heel. You think she's not worthy of being here. I tell you it's because of her great sin, and great repentance that she has every right to come to me.

"Never have I been shown such extravagant love as she has shown me! Trust me, Simon, when I tell you, her faith and repentance have brought about her salvation. All the sanctimonious, holier-than-thou attitudes in the world will never do the same for anyone, including you."

BIBLE REFERENCE: Luke 7:36–39, 44–47 TPT

36 Afterward, a Jewish religious leader named Simon asked Jesus to his home for dinner. Jesus accepted the invitation. When he went to Simon's home, he took his place at the table.

37 In the neighborhood there was an immoral woman of the streets, known to all to be a prostitute. When she heard about Jesus being in Simon's house, she took an exquisite flask made from alabaster, filled it with the most expensive perfume, went right into the home of the Jewish religious leader, and knelt at the feet of Jesus in front of all the guests. **38** Broken and weeping, she covered his feet with the tears that fell from her face. She kept crying and drying his feet with her long hair. Over and over she kissed Jesus' feet. Then she opened her flask and anointed his feet with her costly perfume as an act of worship.

39 When Simon saw what was happening, he thought, "This man can't be a true prophet. If he were really a prophet, he would know what kind of sinful woman is touching him."

44 Then he spoke to Simon about the woman still weeping at his feet.

"Don't you see this woman kneeling here? She is doing for me what you didn't bother to do. When I entered your home as your guest, you didn't think about offering me water to wash the dust off my feet. Yet she came into your home and washed my feet with her many tears and then dried my feet with her hair. **45** You didn't even welcome me into your home with the customary kiss of greeting, but from the moment I came in she has not stopped kissing my feet. **46** You didn't take the time to anoint my head with fragrant oil, but she anointed my head and feet with the finest perfume. **47** She has been forgiven of all her many sins. This is why she has shown me such extravagant love. But those who assume they have very little to be forgiven will love me very little."

What does repentance look like?
How do you distinguish genuine emotion from false?
How do you respond to each one?

Mustard Seeds and Mountains

"What's going on?" Jesus called out as he approached a group of people swarming around a few of his followers. "Is somebody hurt?"

The group parted at his voice. In the center stood Matthew, Andrew, and Philip to one side, and a man with a young boy on the other. It only took a glance at the father's tears to see he was distraught, and the boy's affliction. The expressions on the disciples' faces were nearly as downcast as the father's.

The set of Jesus's jaw and tone of his voice made his authority clear to everyone. The father shuffled slowly toward Jesus and knelt in front of him. His looks at the rest of the group sent them backing up, way up.

"Teacher, my son is very sick. It throws him into horrible convulsions. He has fallen repeatedly into fire and into water. I'm so afraid it will kill him."

"What do you want me to do for him?"

The father shook his head and swiped at his tears with his sleeve. If this was Jesus the healer, how could he not know what he wanted? He took a deep breath and started over, "Jesus, I brought my son to your disciples for healing, but they couldn't do anything."

Jesus reached out a hand to help the father stand up, then pulled him to his side. Jesus's gentle embrace belied the steel in his voice when he turned to his disciples, "What is the deal, people? Haven't you been paying attention? Sometimes I just don't know about you! Bring the boy over here!"

Jesus let go of the father and dropped his hands to the boy's shoulders. Looking straight into the boy's eyes, he told the epilepsy to be gone . . . and it was. Now it was Jesus who knelt as the boy crumpled into his arms. No one moved. No one spoke. The only sounds were the father's quiet sobs, and what sounded like Jesus faintly crooning to the boy.

Keeping one arm around the boy, Jesus finally stood and held out his other arm to draw the father into a group hug.

"Ezra, come," the father whispered to the child. "Let us go tell your mother this wonderful thing Jesus has done for you."

"Boy, will she be surprised!" the boy grinned.

"And thankful, Ezra! We can all be thankful for what Jesus has done for us today," the father said as he smiled and turned toward home with his son.

Neighbors and townspeople didn't know whether to stay or to go. They'd seen the child healed, but Act Two of the prophet's visit might be even more interesting. It looked like his disciples were in for it.

"Matthew, Andrew, Philip, we need to have a word," Jesus said in a low gravelly voice. "The rest of you too." As the followers gathered around him, Jesus turned his gaze on the bystanders. In ones and twos, they began to slip away.

"Master, we tried, honestly we did," Andrew spoke up, elbowing Matthew and Philip.

"We did, we prayed over the boy, we laid hands on him like we've watched you do ..." Matthew put in.

"But, Jesus, nothing happened..." Philip added.

"Yeah, Jesus, nothing, nada..." Matthew said.

"That's enough! We have lived together, eaten together, been driven out of towns together. And we've prayed together. Of all the times you heard me pray to our heavenly Father, did you ever hear a note of doubt in my voice?" Jesus examined the faces of each man. "Well, did you?" Jesus said, his voice beginning to lose its edge.

"No, we didn't. But Master, we're still new to this," Peter rubbed his hands, then his beard.

Jesus's shoulders dropped and he let out a sigh. The disciples glanced up; more than one thought he suddenly seemed tired.

"Here's the deal, guys. You don't have to be a Moses or a Joseph to get your prayers answered," Jesus said, bending down to pick up a tiny pebble. "You see this? If your faith is this tiny, or as small as mustard seed, you can still tell a mountain to move, *and it will*. It's not wizardry; it's cause and effect. If you have even a little faith, God—you know, the Creator of the Universe—will do great things with it."

The teacher and his students stood quietly for a minute letting the lesson get down deep inside them. Then somebody coughed. And somebody else's stomach growled. Then somebody laughed. Pretty soon there was a lot of shoulder bumping, elbows to the ribs, and back patting, and everyone laughing as joy and confidence began to replace doubt and uncertainty.

"Peter, James, John, how about you three go see about getting us something to eat? And make it snappy: we've got more places to go and people to heal!"

BIBLE REFERENCE: Matthew 17:14–21 Contemporary English Version

14 Jesus and his disciples returned to the crowd. A man knelt in front of him **15** and said, "Lord, have pity on my son! He has a bad case of epilepsy and often falls into a fire or into water. **16** I brought him to your disciples, but none of them could heal him."

17 Jesus said, "You people are too stubborn to have any faith! How much longer must I be with you? Why do I have to put up with you? Bring the boy here." **18** Then Jesus spoke sternly to the demon. It went out of the boy, and right then he was healed.

19 Later the disciples went to Jesus in private and asked him, "Why couldn't we force out the demon?"

20–21 Jesus replied:

It is because you don't have enough faith! But I can promise you this. If you had faith no larger than a mustard seed, you could tell this mountain to move from here to there. And it would. Everything would be possible for you.

*Think about the last time your patience was worn thin,
or completely out? Did your sense of urgency
or frustration increase with each failed attempt to make
your message clear? How did you react?*

The Ones Who Get It

"Jesus, aren't you ready for a break yet?" Nathaniel asked, looking around for a place to sit.

"A break from what, Nathaniel? Doing what I came to do?" Jesus said, winking at a small, round face peeking around the corner of the room.

"Don't you see all the people trying to crowd in here?" Philip asked, trying to block the doorway.

"Guys, guys! Give it a rest, will you? These people aren't here to hurt me."

"Master, the Pharisees who just tried to trip you up probably aren't even out of the courtyard yet. You know Herod is running the show here. Have you forgotten all the upheaval your cousin, John the Baptist, caused with pretty much everyone who had any power, like Herod? And look at what happened to him." Peter paced the room like he was addressing troops before a battle.

"Peter! I know far better than you about subversion and plans for evil," Jesus said through clenched teeth, then stood so abruptly the bench he was sitting on crashed to the floor.

"Teacher, we don't understand why we seem to constantly move between conflict and full-on danger. Do you remember where we came from? Some days it's hard to see the point of all this . . . Jesus, are you listening?" John said, gently touching the Teacher's sleeve.

"How about this: you fellows take a break, get a bite to eat. I'm going to hang out here for a little while chatting with folks, then I'll try to explain it to you again," Jesus said to his group of followers, then bent down to wave at the face still peaking around the corner.

Amid mumbling and head wagging, some of the men headed outside. A handful were looking over the humble buffet the homeowners had put out, while the others crashed wherever they could find a seat. As followers went outside, neighbors pushed their way in.

"Mom! The man winked at me, then waved at me," a small voice exploded as his mom scooped him up from the doorway and made her way to where Jesus sat.

"Sir," she whispered, "we've heard stories of the amazing things you've done." She paused and looked over her shoulder. Still holding her squirming son, she whispered, "Would you mind blessing my boy? Is that too much to ask?"

"Daughter, our heavenly Father sees your faith. He loves you the same way you love your child. It would be a pleasure to bless this little guy!" Jesus grinned, putting one hand on the boy's head, and the other on the mother's.

As mother and child were leaving, the boy broke loose and ran to Jesus for a high five. Jesus laughed out loud.

The sound of laughter drew more people into the already crowded room. Whispers of Jesus blessing the boy caused parents to peel clinging kids from their cloaks and robes, and lift them up in their arms.

"Teacher, bless my child too!"

"Jesus, my daughter is ill. Bless her!"

"Master, will you bless my son too?"

Coming back into the room, Simon and Judas muscled their way through the people just as Matthew and Philip left their seats to move toward Jesus.

"People, give Jesus some room! And get those kids outta here. What are you thinking, bringing them in here to see the Master?" Peter rumbled like thunder from behind Jesus.

Quickly standing with a back like a ramrod and a voice like iron, Jesus said, "No, Peter! Men of God, stand down! What are you thinking! Let the kids come to me, all of them. Don't ever get between me and them again, do you understand? Kids are the ones who get it, they really get it. They know who to trust and how to love, can't you see that? Unless you can do the same, you'll never enter the Kingdom."

The room was silent as a stone . . . until tiny fingers tugged on Jesus's hand. Parents gasped. Followers of Jesus tried to fade into walls.

"Jesus, that was funny!" she giggled. "You made those big, loud men scared. I'm not scared, Jesus. I saw you smile too. Can I have a hug now?"

Jesus grinned all over his face as his new friend jumped into his arms while parents and followers watched with eyes wide with amazement and laughter seeping past their lips.

BIBLE REFERENCE: Mark 10:13–16 The Passion Translation

13 The parents kept bringing their little children to Jesus so that he would lay his hands on them *and bless them*. But the disciples kept rebuking and scolding the people for doing it. **14** When Jesus saw what was happening, he became indignant with his disciples and said to them, "Let all the little children come to me and never hinder them! Don't you know that God's kingdom realm exists for such as these? **15** Listen to the truth I speak: Whoever does not open their arms to receive God's kingdom as a teachable child will never enter it." **16** Then he embraced each child, and laying his hands on them, he lovingly blessed each one.

Think about a time when someone completely missed a point you have been trying to make. How many times and ways did you try to explain it? Did you ever reach a point when you were ready to quit trying?

All That Money Can Buy

The motley crew of men straggled out of the small, packed house. Some grabbed a hunk of bread for the road; a couple took a last swig of wine. One was tucking a leather bag into his cloak as he elbowed his way through the crowd. The last man to leave left with only a look of satisfaction on his face.

Waiting outside the door, Judas clutched the leather moneybag and nearly pounced on their leader. "Jesus, are you crazy? Why were you wasting time on those kids? They don't have a single coin to add to our ministry," Judas sneered.

"What are you talking about, Judas?" asked Matthew, the former tax-collector/extortionist cut in. "Don't you know anything about money besides counting it?" Looking around at his friends, Matthew held out a handful of coins. "Am I the only one those excited parents handed offerings to?"

Several others gathered around to toss the coins they'd received into the leather pouch that Judas eagerly opened. The leader of the group stood back watching the scene play out. He chuckled to himself, thinking this was like a pop quiz on one of the basics he'd been trying to teach them.

James slowly dropped his coins into the bag, then put his hand on Judas's shoulder. "Lighten up, Judas! Have we missed a meal yet? Haven't we always had a place to catch a few winks?"

"Yeah, Judas, weren't you listening when Jesus told us about the birds and grass? Remember how he told us flat out that if God takes care of them, He's bound to take care of us," Andrew said. "And He has! Just take a look at this big lout of a brother of mine. Does Peter look like he's been missing any meals?"

Jesus laughed then joined the group, patting first one then another on the back. "Well done, friends, well done! You have been listening and learning about what's important in the eyes of God."

Jerking the purse strings tight on the collected coins, Judas hissed at them, "One of these days all of you'll find out just how valuable money is."

"That's enough of that for now, Judas. Let's see what this young man is in a huff about, shall we?" Jesus said. "Catch your breath, friend, we're not in a hurry. What can we do for you?" Jesus said, reaching a hand out to steady the man.

Holding his side and gasping for breath, the young man started to speak, "Teacher . . . I've been . . . trying to catch up with you."

"Why don't we sit down on the benches over there? Looks like there's a little shade," Jesus told him.

"Thanks, that would be great,"

The two men made themselves comfortable on the nearby benches, while the other men leaned on doorways or simply sat on the ground around them.

"Teacher, I got to listen to you in the synagogue and lots of people are talking about you. I want to know what I have to do to get this thing called eternal life." Everything about his posture showed that the man was eager for an answer.

"First off, do you know the rules of law? You know, about lying, stealing, murder, adultery?"

"Sure, I do," the young man jerked his head around and answered, "I've been trying to follow the rules all my life!"

It was easy to see the man was wealthy by the cut and fabric of his clothes, the jewels on his hands. Still, something about him told Jesus he was sincere. His enthusiasm showed all over his face; he looked like he might launch off the bench any second. The truth was going to be as hard to say, as it was going to be for this seeker to hear.

"I'm really proud of you, just as our heavenly Father is, but he asks one thing more. He asks a great sacrifice of you," Jesus said as he leaned into the young man.

"My father and I go to Jerusalem frequently, and we always make sacrifices as prescribed by the law. What else must I sacrifice?"

"Everything."

"But, Jesus..." the young man whispered, looking around at Jesus's followers and hoping he'd misheard.

"I know. Maybe it seems impossible, but if you really want to be a part of God's kingdom you have to be willing to get rid of everything that represents the kingdom of earth."

The young man's head dropped into his hands and his shoulders began to shake. The men watching didn't know if he was going to snap or dissolve into a crying mess. Jesus slowly put his hand on the man's shoulder.

No one said a word. The shade was beginning to move away from the benches.

Finally, the young man lifted and shook his head. With great effort, as though a rack of bricks had been placed on his back, he stood and walked away.

Like a sudden gust of air before a rising storm, the followers let out a collective breath.

"Judas, Matthew, James, all of you, do you have any idea how hard it is for the wealthy to enter Kingdom living? Sure, money has its perks, but it also has its pitfalls and distractions. You can't imagine how hard it is to walk away from a wealthy lifestyle!

"Do you see that camel the young man is getting on? It would be easier for it to pass through the eye of the needle that sewed your clothes than for him to give all he owns to the poor and serve God only."

Jesus slowly stood up. "Look, guys, I'm running out of time. I've never sugarcoated any of the truth my heavenly Father sent me to share, and I'm not going to start this late in the game. I know you gave up a lot to follow me. I wish I could tell you it's going to get easier, but that would be a lie.

"Right here, right now, this is what I want you to know: kingdom living is two-pronged. First, and most importantly, it's keeping your eyes on the prize by being obedient to our Father, living for him. Secondly, kingdom living means living for others.

"I also promise two things. It's going to be an uphill battle all the way. But here's the great news, so don't miss it, *you never have to do it alone.* Now, it's time to hunker down and head to Jerusalem."

And that's just what he did while his mixed up, messy band of followers walked silently behind.

BIBLE REFERENCE: Mark 10:17–25 The Message

17 As he went out into the street, a man came running up, greeted him with great reverence, and asked, "Good Teacher, what must I do to get eternal life?"

18–19 Jesus said, "Why are you calling me good? No one is good, only God. You know the commandments: Don't murder, don't commit adultery, don't steal, don't lie, don't cheat, honor your father and mother."

20 He said, "Teacher, I have—from my youth—kept them all!"

21 Jesus looked him hard in the eye—and loved him! He said, "There's one thing left: Go sell whatever you own and give it to the poor. All your wealth will then be heavenly wealth. And come follow me."

22 The man's face clouded over. This was the last thing he expected to hear, and he walked off with a heavy heart. He was holding on tight to a lot of things, and not about to let go.

23–25 Looking at his disciples, Jesus said, "Do you have any idea how difficult it is for people who 'have it all' to enter God's kingdom?" The disciples couldn't believe what they were hearing, but Jesus kept on: "You can't imagine how difficult. I'd say it's easier for a camel to go through a needle's eye than for the rich to get into God's kingdom."

*Was there a time you had to tell someone
something that was hard to hear?
How did the exchange make you feel?*

Can't Keep a Good Man Down!

The footsteps of the disciples became heavier and heavier. What a day it had been! First Jesus played with some kids, then he told his followers they had to be like little kids to get into heaven. They were still trying to choke that down and hadn't even cleared the city limits when the young rich guy ambushed Jesus. Jesus's lesson from that little gabfest was that it's preferable to be poor. Go figure! Snippets of conversations floated on the air…

"Who knew Jesus was crazy about kids! I don't get all that stuff about becoming childlike…" Thomas said, shaking his head.

"Obviously Jesus doesn't care how we get the bills paid. Better to be poor, huh? In what world?" Judas complained.

"I'm worried about Jesus's talk about a trial and being executed. Where does that leave the rest of us?" Philip asked Nathaniel.

If laying all that good news on his followers wasn't tough enough, Jesus told them they were on the way to Jerusalem for those unimaginable events to take place.

And now, just to add to all of that madness, James and John were trying to get on the inside track with Jesus, asking to be with him in the mix when Jesus came into power. Just because they were some of the first ones recruited by Jesus didn't make them any better than anyone else.

What's next? With their brains on overload, and their spirits dragging the ground, Jesus's followers were silent as they walked down the dusty road. Their silence did nothing to discourage others from joining them along the way, many talking about their recent healings. Soon the road was lined with people from the next village hoping to be healed.

"Jesus! Jesus is that you? You, Son of David, and the Living God! I need your touch!" A voice rose above the chatter of the increasing number of people crowding the sides of the road.

"Pipe down, Bartimaeus! The Master doesn't have time for a beggar like you," a man next to him snapped.

"But it's Jesus! Don't you get it? They say he can heal anyone!"

"Come on, Bartimaeus! Can't you see these men are worn out? Give it a rest," quipped another bystander.

The beggar's shoulders dropped as he began to melt into the crowd.

"John, did I hear someone calling me?" Jesus asked, stopping in his tracks.

"Maybe. We seem to draw a crowd wherever we go. It could have been anyone," the disciple answered.

Jesus turned to one of the men beside the road. "Did you hear someone call my name? Did you see who it was?"

"It may have been 'blind' Bartimaeus. He sits out here by the road nearly every day begging from travelers," the man said, pointing into the growing crowd. "He's the one wearing the tattered cloak."

"Quick! Tell him to come to me," Jesus said, stretching up to try and see someone wearing a tattered cloak.

"But, Mast..." John began, touching Jesus's arm.

Jesus jerked his arm away, briefly glancing at John, then turning back to the crowd "I said, BRING BARTIMAEUS TO ME!"

As if they were one, the crowd gasped at the authority of Jesus, then parted before him. Near the back of the group of people, a man in a tattered cloak stopped and turned at the sound of his name, as Jesus waited for the blind man to come.

"Jesus, I'm here! I'm here, Son of God!" Bartimaeus called. He stumbled in the direction of the voice, his arms flailing about. "I'm coming, Jesus! Wait for me!" Bartimaeus called out again, his voice becoming shrill in his desperation not to miss his Savior.

"Bartimaeus, my friend, I'm right here!" Jesus said, as though soothing a child. "What can I do for you?" he asked, laying a hand on Bartimaeus's shoulder.

"Oh, Teacher, if only I could see! I know you can heal me," Bartimaeus replied, his voice trembling, and dissolving into a whisper.

"No problem, Friend, you have already done the hard part. Your faith has healed you!" Jesus said, grinning broadly.

With a shake of his head and a shout for joy, Bartimaeus reached out and put his hand on Jesus's. "Master, your cloak is dark and your tunic is light! Jesus, I can see everything! Jesus! I can see your smile sparkling your eyes."

"It does indeed! And I can show you even more. Do you see the man in the cloak the color of leaves over there? If you'd like to join us, Nathaniel will walk with you," Jesus said, waving for Nathaniel to join him and his newest follower.

"Join you. Join you? Are you kidding? Jesus, you gave me my sight and my life! Nothing would make me happier than to give it back to you."

Looking around at his closest friends, Jesus saw smiles begin to overtake their grim faces. Peter laughed loudly and slapped Andrew on the back. Though Jesus had temporarily rebuffed him, John now smiled and nodded at him. Jesus waited for the excitement of Bartimaeus's healing to percolate through the group, then motioned for them to huddle around him.

"It's been a long, roller-coaster ride kind of day, hasn't it?" Jesus asked as he looked deep into the faces of his followers. "I praise our heavenly Father that we can end the day on a high note. There are two things I want you to always remember, especially in the days just ahead. First, *never underestimate the power of God*. And second," Jesus paused, and invited Bartimaeus to stand by his side, *"there's always room in the Kingdom for one more."*

With lighter steps and a hum of joy and excitement, Jesus and his believers headed back down the road.

BIBLE REFERENCE: Mark 10:46– 52 The Living Bible

46 And so they reached Jericho. Later, as they left town, a great crowd was following. Now it happened that a blind beggar named Bartimaeus (the son of Timaeus) was sitting beside the road as Jesus was going by.

47 When Bartimaeus heard that Jesus from Nazareth was near, he began to shout out, "Jesus, Son of David, have mercy on me!"

48 "Shut up!" some of the people yelled at him.

But he only shouted the louder, again and again, "O Son of David, have mercy on me!"

49 When Jesus heard him, he stopped there in the road and said, "Tell him to come here."

So they called the blind man. "You lucky fellow," they said, "come on, he's calling you!" **50** Bartimaeus yanked off his old coat and flung it aside, jumped up and came to Jesus.

51 "What do you want me to do for you?" Jesus asked.

"O Teacher," the blind man said, "I want to see!"

52 And Jesus said to him, "All right, it's done. Your faith has healed you."

And instantly the blind man could see and followed Jesus down the road!

What's the hardest, best change you can imagine for your life? What would it take to make it happen? What makes you hesitate in taking the next step toward it?

Come Out!

The banks of the river were crowded. Even though Jesus's cousin, John the Baptist, had been executed by Herod, there were still those who flocked to one of John's favorite stomping grounds. The gentle current of the Jordan River was soothing. Tree-lined banks offered shade to weary pilgrims.

"Jesus, I think there's room for all of us over here," called James, dropping a basket of fruit and cheese on the ground.

"Could you say that a little louder, James?" asked his brother John. "I thought we were trying to keep a low profile."

"It's okay, John. James was only trying to help," the group's leader said.

"Yeah, John, it's not like people don't always show up wherever Jesus is," Peter said, tossing his cloak beside the fruit basket. "As long as they aren't hauling rocks for stoning, like the Jewish big shots we escaped a couple of days ago, it's all good. Right, Jesus?" Peter continued, sprawling on his cloak and grabbing a fig.

"Right, Peter. James, this is a great place for lunch. Who's got the bread?"

The small band of teacher and followers were nearly finished eating when they saw a young man running in their direction.

Stopping abruptly by Jesus, the man leaned over to catch his breath. "Are you . . . are you Jesus?"

"I am. How can I help you?"

"Your friends, Mary and Martha, sent me to find and tell you Lazarus is really sick. They're afraid he'll die and asked you to come right away," the messenger told Jesus and his men.

"Sit, rest a moment. Eat something. I know you must be tired from your journey," Jesus encouraged him. "When you're rested, you can return to tell Mary and Martha I'll be there as soon as possible."

"Jesus, it's going to take us nearly a day to get to Bethany. Do you think we better hit the road first thing tomorrow?" Peter questioned Jesus.

"Peter, I'm really hoping you'll figure out I've got things under control much sooner than later. We'll head over to Bethany when I say, not a minute sooner. If I'm not worried about Lazarus, you don't need to be either. You got it?"

"But Lord..."

"My way or the highway, Peter. It's that simple," Jesus said, getting up and heading toward the crowd.

After devouring fruit and cheese, the messenger was on his way. Knowing Mary and Martha weren't going to like his message, he wasn't moving too quickly. The disciples watched him leave then turned their attention to Jesus working the crowd. One by one the disciples began to seek out those in need.

For two more days visitors to the Jordan River came and went while Jesus and his followers comforted, prayed with, and healed those who had come looking for a respite from sickness and worry.

"Get your stuff together, brothers! It's time to go to Bethany," Jesus told the men the third day after they received the message from Mary and Martha.

The trip to Bethany made for a long day. The only one who didn't seem tense was Jesus. The closer they got to Bethany, the less the men talked. The disciples had probably seen Jesus heal hundreds of people, but this was different. Lazarus and his sisters were friends of theirs and Jesus. Since they began following Jesus, they had probably spent more time with this small family than anyone else.

The group of men was drawing close to the turn off to Lazarus's house when they began to hear the mourners.

"This can't be good," Peter muttered to Andrew. "These paid mourners can only mean that Lazarus has died . . . we didn't make it in time."

"I know, this is going to tax Jesus in more ways than one."

From the back of the group, Peter and Andrew saw John step closer to Jesus and begin to match his pace.

"Jesus, it looks like we may be headed into the lion's den. What do you want us to do?"

There was a slight twinge in Jesus's jaw. "Nothing, John, nothing. I've got to do this myself," Jesus answered, never taking his eyes from the wailing mourners.

"What a huge waste of money! Paying mourners!" Judas sneered to no one in particular.

Sidling up to him, James elbowed Judas in the ribs and said, "Might not be such a bad idea, Judas. You know some poor schmucks might not have any mourners otherwise. Know what I mean?"

"You think you're so funny, don't you, James?" Judas snarled, jerking away from him.

"Seriously, James?" asked Peter, pulling James aside. "I'm usually the dense one, but it doesn't take a prophet or scholar to know everybody's nerves are on edge."

"I was just kidding, Peter. Lighten up, why don't you?"

"Not today, James. And neither should you. One of our friends has died, and I really don't know how Jesus is going to react to Mary and Martha."

"Guess we're going to find out. Here comes Mary now."

The disciples stopped alongside the road unsure of what to expect as the scene of mourning began to play out in front of them. Jesus was approaching the house, moving through the mob of real and not-so-real mourners.

"Jesus! You're finally here!" Mary exclaimed, nearly knocking Jesus over as she fell at his feet.

Her hair and clothes disheveled and her tear-smeared face a hot mess, Mary didn't look at all like the woman of serenity and grace who had chosen to sit and learn at Jesus's feet during their last visit.

"Lord, how could you let Lazarus die?" she asked, tugging on his robe. "We just knew if you'd been here you could have saved him..." Mary's words faded away as she clung to Jesus.

Pulling her up by her hands, Jesus looked around and saw friends and neighbors he'd met on his visits to Mary's home. The rejection and grief in their faces and postures were almost more than he could take. Had the men not been taught about the resurrection after death in the synagogue, and shared it with their families? Had visitors to Mary's home not listened as he shared the same message? Was it some obscure scripture lesson to them?

"Mary, where is Lazarus?"

"Lord, he's in the tomb, of course."

"Show me," Jesus said, his voice low and prickly.

The mourners and neighbors were only too willing to show this teacher, this supposed healer where Lazarus had been laid. Other interested parties had begun to infiltrate the group as word spread to Jewish leaders that Jesus was back in town. Maybe, just maybe, they would catch him violating Mosaic law, or better yet, blaspheming.

Mary held tightly to Jesus's hand as they walked toward the tomb. Her closest friends formed a barrier between them and the paid crowd. Their friend's love for Lazarus and his sisters was as obvious as their sorrow. Jesus's shoulders began to shake as they came in sight of the tomb. He gave Mary a quick hug, and as he milled about the group of friends, some said they saw tears running down his face.

Comments began to rumble on the fringes of those most devoted to the family.

"Wow, guess Jesus really cared about Lazarus; even he's crying!"

"Maybe so, but if he was all that, why didn't he show up before now?"

"Yeah, they say Jesus healed all kinds of people. You'd think he'd do the same for his 'friends'."

"What does he expect to do now? The guy's dead, for crying out loud."

Jesus went to the stone that had been placed over the entrance to the tomb and placed his hand on it. For a minute he just stood there, his head bowed, tears splattering onto his sandals.

Suddenly, with the precision of a soldier, Jesus threw back his shoulders and straightened to his full height. No more tears, only a fierceness in his eyes as if he were going to battle.

Without turning his head, Jesus called out in a voice that demanded attention, *"Roll away the stone . . . now!"*

Pushing through the crowd of the sincere and the charlatans, Martha rushed to Jesus.

"Jesus, no!" she said, grabbing his sleeve. "Lord, please, Lazarus has been dead for four days; the odor will be horrible!" she whispered, dipping her head.

Finally, Jesus turned to Martha, "Martha, were you so busy taking care of the house whenever I came that you didn't bother to listen when I told you that you hadn't seen anything yet? I've got more power than you can possibly imagine and I promised that you would see it revealed. Now, get a grip and go stand by your sister; you're not going to want to miss this!"

Mary ran to where Jesus and her sister had been talking. She grabbed Martha's hand and gently pulled her to the side.

"I said, 'Roll away the stone.' What are you waiting for?" Jesus barked at the men who stood hesitating by the tomb.

Most of the crowd fell silent at the authority in Jesus's voice. Most, but not all. A small group of temple leaders smirked, whispered among themselves, and one was even seen rubbing his hands together. Friends, neighbors, and even paid mourners wagged their heads at what appeared to be disrespect for the dead as they slowly inched away from those who held power in the synagogue and the community.

All eyes were fixed on the One they had been waiting to come. Lazarus was dead; what more could be done?

"Father, I know you are listening and will answer my prayer for my friend, Lazarus. Let me bring you glory so that those who are here will know beyond a shadow of a doubt that you sent me," Jesus said, his face lifted up.

He turned toward the open tomb, and in a loud voice commanded, *"Lazarus! Come out!"*

BIBLE REFERENCE: John 11:32–44 The Passion Translation

32 When Mary finally found Jesus outside the village, she fell at his feet in tears and said, "Lord, if only you had been here, my brother would not have died."

33 When Jesus looked at Mary and saw her weeping at his feet, and all her friends who were with her grieving, he shuddered with emotion[a] and was deeply moved with tenderness and compassion. **34** He said to them, "Where did you bury him?"

"Lord, come with us and we'll show you," they replied.

35 Then tears streamed down Jesus' face.

36 Seeing Jesus weep caused many of the mourners to say, "Look how much he loved Lazarus." **37** Yet others said, "Isn't this the One who opens blind eyes? Why didn't he do something to keep Lazarus from dying?"

38 Then Jesus, with intense emotions, came to the tomb—a cave with a stone placed over its entrance. **39** Jesus told them, "Roll away the stone."

Then Martha said, "But Lord, it's been four days since he died—by now his body is already decomposing!"

40 Jesus looked at her and said, "Didn't I tell you that if you'll believe in me, you'll see God unveil his power?"

41 So they rolled away the heavy stone. Jesus gazed into heaven and said, "Father, thank you that you have heard my prayer, **42** for you listen to every word I speak. Now, so that these who stand here with me will believe that you have sent me to the earth as your messenger, *I will use the power you have given me.*" **43** Then with a loud voice Jesus shouted with authority: "Lazarus! Come out of the tomb!"

44 Then in front of everyone, Lazarus, who had died four days earlier, slowly hobbled out—he still had grave clothes tightly wrapped around his hands and feet and covering his face! Jesus said to them, "Unwrap him and let him loose."

---

a. John 11:33 The Greek word used here (*enebrimēsato*) can also mean "indignant and stirred with anger." Was he angry at the mourners? Not at all. He was angry over the work of the devil in taking the life of his friend, Lazarus. (The Aramaic, however, has no connotation of indignation, only tenderness and compassion (lit. "his heart melted with compassion").

*Friendship can be a risky business.
Have you ever experienced so much disappointment
in a friend's actions that it caused grief or sorrow?*

Don't Cry for Me

"Philip, did you and Thomas talk to anyone when you went into town for the colt Jesus wanted?" Peter asked.

"Don't you trust us, Peter? Jesus said not to talk to anyone unless they asked about us taking it and that's what we did," Philip retorted.

"So, where do you think all of these people are coming from?" James asked. "Did we miss the parade memo?"

"Come on, guys, haven't you figured out there's a pattern, a correlation between Jesus and the crowds?" John asked. "I'm convinced there's a big picture plan in progress here. There's nothing new about having lots of people around."

"Not like this. What's up with the palm branches and people tossing their robes on the ground?" James scratched his beard and looked around at the gathering crowd.

"This is just weird," Peter said, shaking his head and lowering his voice. "You know Jerusalem will be crawling with bigwigs and Roman soldiers. They're all trying to catch us regular guys breaking some kind of rule or regulation."

"Peter's right," John said. "This crowd isn't going to go unnoticed."

"Not to mention Jesus is spoiling for a fight," Judas hissed.

Peter moved toward Judas until he towered over him. "Not near as much as you, Judas!" he said under his breath.

"You can't bully me, Peter! You're not in charge. Nobody is. We thought we were following some great leader who was going to free us from the Romans, and look who we got? An itinerant preacher on a donkey!" Judas retorted, puffing out his chest.

Andrew stepped between the two men just as Peter raised his fist. Judas smirked and quickly stepped to the side of the road.

As the group neared the gates of Jerusalem, the crowd grew. Children ran and danced waving palms their parents handed them. Young boys threw palm branches on the road and were followed by maidens laying robes and blankets on top of them as the donkey and its rider rode by. The festive atmosphere bordered on mania.

"Peter, Andrew, Philip...I think we need to get closer to Jesus," John called over the noise of the growing mob. "Grab the others; there's no telling what could happen."

The gang of twelve, minus Judas, quickly infiltrated the crowd closest to Jesus, one placing a hand on the donkey's head, and another on its rump. Maybe it was Jesus being jostled by the throng of followers, or the bumpy road, but Andrew would have sworn Jesus was shaking. He pushed his way next to the rider and animal with one hand, while motioning to Peter to do the same on the other side of Jesus.

Jesus and his followers were nearly at the gate when he began to shake his head. When he turned and saw Peter, he said, "They have no idea. Things could have been so different and now it's too late."

"It's too late for what, Jesus?"

Jesus wagged his head, slinging tears across his shoulders, splattering onto Peter's arm as he reached out to steady his teacher. Jesus glanced at Peter as sobs shook his whole frame.

"Jesus…

"Jerusalem, you have denied the gift sent by your heavenly Father. Because you have forsaken Him, He will forsake you to your enemies. He has called you joyful, the city of truth and of faith, and yet because you chose to turn down the gift of peace, He has offered you, your enemies will totally demolish you…" Jesus's voice dwindled as tears continued to run down and drip from his beard.

"Jesus? Jesus! You've got to get a grip! Don't you see all the soldiers starting to mingle with the people? One of them might hear you," Peter said, shaking Jesus's arm.

"Come on, Jesus," Andrew called to him from the head of the donkey. "You don't want anyone to get hurt. Just look at the faces on those Pharisees and scribes; they mean business."

The jammed streets of Jerusalem and heightened presence of Roman soldiers brought a halt to the parade. Palms were hastily dropped. Robes clasped tightly. Children reached frantically for parents' hands. Voices and faces raised in song and celebration lost their joy.

The donkey slowly stopped. Its rider gathered his robes around him and slid to the ground. He drug a sleeve across his face and straightened his shoulders. Without turning or saying a word, eleven men swarmed around him, and the crowd ahead of them parted as they headed for the Temple.

BIBLE REFERENCE: John 11:41–44 The Living Bible

41 But as they came closer to Jerusalem and he saw the city ahead, he began to cry. **42** "Eternal peace was within your reach and you turned it down," he wept, "and now it is too late. **43** Your enemies will pile up earth against your walls and encircle you and close in on you, **44** and crush you to the ground, and your children within you; your enemies will not leave one stone upon another—for you have rejected the opportunity God offered you."

> *Recall a time someone you cared deeply for did something you felt sure she would regret. Did you intervene? How was your relationship changed?*
>
>

Stay in Your Lane

"Jesus, how did you score this sweet deal?" Peter said around a mouthful of lamb and bread.

"Couth up, Peter, and keep your mouth shut while you're eating!" Andrew told him, throwing a stiff elbow to Peter's ribs.

"Andrew's right, Peter," said Matthew. "But for real, Jesus, how did you swing this? It's not our usual midweek spread."

"And what a huge waste of money," Judas grumbled, having returned to the group after the parade into Jerusalem. No one bothered to question his absence

"Judas, why can't you enjoy anything without worrying about the money? Haven't you listened to anything Jesus has tried to teach us?" John asked, reaching for another piece of cheese and hunk of bread.

"Jesus," Peter said, now with his mouth empty, "you still haven't told us how you pulled this all off."

"Haven't I, Peter?" Jesus paused, taking a slow drink of wine. "Oh well, let's just say I know who to go to in order to get our needs met."

The teacher and his followers ate and drank, enjoying the camaraderie they had built over the last three years. The meal in a quiet room was one to be savored after several long and busy days. Many had been healed and listened attentively to Jesus's teachings, but since coming to Jerusalem the air seemed to pulsate with tension. At some point during the evening, Judas had silently slipped away.

As plates and cups emptied, Jesus dropped out of the conversation. He seemed to withdraw into himself. Finally, he got up from the table. He took off his robe and wrapped a towel around his waist as a servant would.

"Jesus, what are you doing?" Philip gasped.

Without saying a word, Jesus went to the side table where he poured water into a basin. Then he went to each man and gently washed the dust from their tired and weary feet.

"Oh, no, Jesus, not me!" Peter said, pulling his feet away.

"Peter, if I don't do this, you have no part of me."

Peter shook his head, while Jesus knelt before him and waited. "But Jesus…" he said as a tear fell and wet his beard.

"It's up to you, Peter. If you want to be a part of me, if you want to truly follow me, then I must wash your feet."

Jutting out his feet and lifting his hands, Peter exclaimed, "Then, Lord, wash all of me!"

Placing one foot into the basin and then the other, Jesus chuckled, "Peter, you've already been washed; you just need a little cleaning up."

In a room where you could hear a pin drop, Jesus finished washing the feet of his disciples. He finally put away the towel and basin, then went back to his seat. He looked lovingly at each face, not quite smiling.

"Here's the deal, guys. We've done amazing things together. We've also suffered hardships and more than a little torment.

As I've said before, I wish I could say things are going to get better . . . but they're not.

"You've called me Teacher, and you're right. Now listen up, this is the game-changer: if I, your Teacher, am willing to do the most lowly of tasks for you, washing your feet, you should be willing to do the same for each other. I only do what our Heavenly Father tells me to do. I expect no less from you.

"You're my beloved disciples, but only if you follow my example and do what God tells you to do. You're no longer your own bosses. If you understand that you're to stay in your lane, and let Him take the lead, you will be blessed."

Jesus settled back into his seat and poured himself another cup of wine. He needed to tell them so much more. It was going to be a long night, and the fewer surprises for them, the better.

BIBLE REFERENCE: John 13:1, 3–5, 12–17 Revised Standard Version

1 Now before the feast of the Passover, when Jesus knew that his hour had come to depart out of this world to the Father, having loved his own who were in the world, he loved them to the end... **3** Jesus, knowing that the Father had given all things into his hands, and that he had come from God and was going to God, **4** rose from supper, laid aside his garments, and girded himself with a towel. **5** Then he poured water into a basin, and began to wash the disciples' feet, and to wipe them with the towel with which he was girded . . .

12 When he had washed their feet, and taken his garments, and resumed his place, he said to them, "Do you know what I have done to you? **13** You call me Teacher and Lord; and you are right, for so I am. **14** If I then, your Lord and Teacher, have washed your feet, you also ought to wash one another's feet. **15** For I have given you an example, that you also should do as I have done to you. **16** Truly, truly, I say to you, a servant is not greater than his master; nor is he who is sent greater than he who sent him. **17** If you know these things, blessed are you if you do them."

> *Service isn't just about hands; it's also about the heart. Sometimes service is down and dirty. Think about a time when you chose to serve someone else despite your lack of enthusiasm for the task.*
>
>

Deserted

The road was packed. Jerusalem was the place to be for the Passover festival. Families, merchants, con men, zealots, and all types of folks with a single goal: get the most out of the Jewish celebration.

Crying babies, restless kids, endless vendors already hawking their wares, Roman soldiers harshly directing traffic. The cacophony of the crowd could have just as easily been in the marketplace or on any other jam-packed Roman road. An edge to the noise echoed the hostility in the courtyard of the governor's palace a few hours earlier in the day.

Amphoras holding new wine whispered a barely perceptible aroma that mingled with fragrances coming from baskets of pungent ginger and olives, all headed for the marketplace. Unfortunately, no amount of delicacies could completely mask the stench of animals and death.

The hill near the road into the Jewish "Holy City" was a prime spot to display Roman expertise in crucifixion. It was meant as a deterrent to those who might be thinking about bucking against the power that ruled the known world. Soldiers seemed unaffected by the display of their handiwork, and openly smirked at those traveling to the city.

The gruesome, tortuous executions filled the air with the foulness of blood and torn bodies. Averting their faces could not erase images of distorted forms from the travelers' minds, or filter out echoes of ragged breaths and moans. Parents drew their children closer, fathers becoming shields against the hatred of heavily armed troops. Mothers did their best to protect their children from the horrific sights and sounds all around them. The road into Jerusalem seemed longer than ever before.

For some among the crowd, the teacher on the middle cross was getting exactly what he deserved. How could he have the arrogance to claim he was the Son of God? A growing number of Pharisees, scribes, and other temple leaders gathered to hurl caustic taunts at this teacher as if stoning him.

As the throng pushed toward the gates of Jerusalem, priests and scribes wound their ways through the crowd. They were careful to stay on the side of the road opposite Roman soldiers; after all, they couldn't risk becoming unclean, especially in plain view of other Jews. Concern about being unclean didn't interfere with the men of the Temple gloating as they gazed upon the criminal in the center of the trio being executed. Their plan for his demise had worked.

BIBLE REFERENCE: Mark 15:29–34 The Living Bible

29–30 The people jeered at him as they walked by, and wagged their heads in mockery.

"Ha! Look at you now!" they yelled at him. "Sure, you can destroy the Temple and rebuild it in three days! If you're so wonderful, save yourself and come down from the cross."

31 The chief priests and religious leaders were also standing around joking about Jesus.

"He's quite clever at 'saving' others," they said, "but he can't save himself!"

32 "Hey there, Messiah!" they yelled at him. "You 'King of Israel'! Come on down from the cross and we'll believe you!"

And even the two robbers dying with him cursed him.

33 About noon, darkness fell across the entire land, lasting until three o'clock that afternoon.

34 Then Jesus called out with a loud voice, *"Eli, Eli, lama sabachthani?"* ("My God, my God, why have you deserted me?")

Being humiliated or deserted is not for the fainthearted.
When it's compounded with doing your best
to help someone else, the pain can become unbearable.
Reflect on a time when you, or someone close to you,
felt forsaken despite best efforts to help others.
How did you fight your way past the pain?

Mother's Day

The small group of soldiers sat on the ground. They seemed oblivious to the excruciating pain of the men just a few feet away.

"I guess with the pittance we get paid for doing the top dog's dirty work, picking up a used garment once in a while is supposed to make us feel better," Gerardo, one of the soldiers, complained to his compatriots.

"At least this guy in the middle has decent clothes, not rags like the other two . . . " Luigi said, tossing the other criminals' clothes onto their small fire.

"Hey, Antonio, let me see that tunic. It looks pretty nice," Bernardo, the third soldier of the quartet said, reaching for the tunic.

"Bernardo, I don't think it has a seam. This is too good to rip apart," Antonio said, handing over the tunic. "Luigi, do you have your bag of stones?"

"Sure, what for?"

"What do you think?" Gerardo growled. "We're going to cast lots for the tunic, that's what for."

While soldiers calmly bargained and cast lots for Jesus's clothes, a disciple and a small group of women inched closer to his cross.

"Look what they've done to my child," Mary, the mother of Jesus moaned, stretching out her hand to gently touch his bleeding feet. As she began to collapse from insurmountable grief, John, the disciple, put his arms around her.

Other hands reached out to her. "Mary, come, come back," her sister-in-law urged her. "Step back so Jesus can see your face."

With her eyes never leaving the face of her son, Mary let John guide her back a short way. Her bloodstained fingers dangled at her side. Mary Magdalene quickly tore a strip from her underskirt and wiped her friend's hand.

Jesus's mother looked sadly at her friend, "Mary, do you see what the soldiers are doing? Do they have no hearts or souls? How can they torture Jesus so cruelly, then gamble for his clothes?"

Tears filled Mary Magdalene's eyes as she watched the men cast lots for the tunic their friend Salome had made for Jesus.

"John, Mary!" the sister-in-law said, grabbing John's sleeve. "Look! Jesus is looking at us!"

John pushed the women behind him as he sidestepped the gamblers and drew closer to the cross.

Parched lips cracked open and a hoarse voice said, "Mother, Mother…"

"Mary, he's calling for you!"

Throwing off hands and words of well-meaning "sisters," Mary stumbled past them and the soldiers.

"Jesus! Son, I'm here, I'm here! Can you see me, Jesus?" Once again, Mary reached up to caress the feet of her son.

"Mother, see John? Now he is your son," Jesus croaked, his words barely audible.

"No…" Mary whispered, burying her face in the rough timber of her son's cross.

It took all the strength of a fisherman's hands and arms to pry her from the blood-soaked wood, wood warmed by the Savior's life blood spilt upon it. John folded Mary into his cloak, adding her pain to his own.

"John…"

Still holding Mary, John turned his face back to the cross. "I'm here, Jesus, I'm here," John whispered, tears rolling down his face.

"John, she is your mother now. Take care of her."

BIBLE REFERENCE: John 19:24–27 The Message

24–27 While the soldiers were looking after themselves, Jesus' mother, his aunt, Mary the wife of Clopas, and Mary Magdalene stood at the foot of the cross. Jesus saw his mother and the disciple he loved standing near her. He said to his mother, "Woman, here is your son." Then to the disciple, "Here is your mother." From that moment the disciple accepted her as his own mother.

> *Great love can demand great sacrifice.*
> *Think about an incident when a sacrifice*
> *was willingly given. What were the*
> *effects of such a love offering?*

Ticket to Paradise

"John, why do they torment my son so? As if their awful torture and this horrendous execution weren't enough? My son has only loved them..." Mary asked, leaning into the arms that Salome offered her.

"Jesus tried to tell us that he would be forsaken, Mary. Maybe that's why he gave you into my care, so you would never feel like you've been left alone," John said, gently touching Mary's hand.

"Mary! John! Listen! Did you hear them? What are the thieves saying to Jesus?" Salome said, pointing to the hideous crosses.

One of the criminals hanging alongside cursed him: "Some Messiah you are! Save yourself! Save us!" But the other one made him shut up: "Have you no fear of God? You're getting the same as him. We deserve this, but not him—he did nothing to deserve this." (Luke 23:39–41 MSG)

"Thank you, Heavenly Father, thank you for words in my son's ear that remind him that you have not deserted him. Thank you . . . " Mary's voice drifted off into silent prayer.

Salome and Mary Magdalene motioned to the other women who had followed Jesus to come closer and join ranks around the mother of their teacher. John stepped closer to the cross and leaned in to hear any word from the dying men.

Then (the thief) said, "Jesus, remember me when you enter your kingdom." (Luke 23:42 MSG)

"Sisters! Look!" John turned and reached out a hand to draw their eyes to the awful sight only a few feet away. "Jesus is pushing up like he's trying to say something. Listen! Come closer!"

Then Jesus said to (the thief), "I promise you, today you'll be with me in paradise." (Luke 23:43 ERV)

"My son!" Mary exclaimed, throwing off the embraces of the women. "How can we hope to love as you love?" Mary cried out, the words torn from her throat, as her friends fell to their knees.
"Lord! Forgive us for not listening... . . . not believing," John fell to his knees.
The small group seemed to implode under the glaring example of divine love. Each one holding an image of their own lackluster devotion to others. Sorrow clung to them as they leaned into one another. How could they go on without Jesus to show them the way to go?

BIBLE REFERENCE: Luke 23:39–43 New Testament for Everyone

39 One of the bad characters who was hanging there began to insult him. 'Aren't you the Messiah?' he said. 'Rescue yourself – and us, too!'

40 But the other one told him off. 'Don't you fear God?' he said. 'You're sharing the same fate that he is! **41** In our case it's fair enough; we're getting exactly what we asked for. But this fellow hasn't done anything out of order.

42 'Jesus,' he went on, 'remember me when you finally become king.'

43 'I'm telling you the truth,' replied Jesus, 'you'll be with me in paradise, this very day.'

> *As humans, we all fail at one time or another.*
> *Most of us have been disappointed in ourselves or others.*
> *Think about a time someone came alongside during*
> *a time of failure or disappointment. How did their efforts*
> *affect your perception of yourself or the situation?*

Missing in Action

Exhaustion was draped around them like a woolen blanket. Their bodies worn out from lack of sleep, terror, and grief. Emotions, raw, set to go off with the slightest injury. Their hearts were broken and minds still reeled from trying to make sense of the last couple of days. There had been no reason to stay in bed and try to sleep.

Weary feet, darkness, and an unfamiliar path made the way treacherous for a lone follower of Jesus. Power and wealth had allowed Joseph of Arimathea and Nicodemus to seek Pilate's permission to claim her Savior's body. The tomb was supposed to be near the abhorrent site of Jesus's death on the cross. A tomb in a garden, perhaps meant to bring some peace and solace to mourners. Instead, its night-blackened silence only added weight to the woman's already heavy spirit.

John's directions were good. That must be the tomb. Joseph's position in the Sanhedrin and with the Roman government assured him of wealth making it possible for him to have a large tomb with a stone much taller than Peter.

Just a couple more steps to the tomb, perhaps a few moments of quiet here in the shrouded garden to let reality settle into her heart that her Savior was dead . . . wait a minute! Did the feeble light of the lantern play tricks on her weary brain? Maybe tired eyes weren't seeing right.

The massive stone was rolled away from the tomb!

As the rays of the sun began to stretch across the horizon, the lantern dropped and feet sped back to the place where the disciples huddled in fear.

She thrust the door open, yelling, "Peter, John . . . the stone has been rolled away from the tomb." Mary Magdalen paused for a moment to catch her breath. "I don't know where Jesus is!"

Stalwart fishermen nearly knocked her over as they ran out the door.

"Wait! I'm coming!" Mary called after the disciples, her lungs screaming for more air, her heart racing ahead of her feet.

Three Christ-followers raced toward the gaping mouth of the tomb, fearful of what they might find.

The mounting sun threw shadows against stones and tombs. Bushes tore at cloaks. Rocks and pebbles slid beneath the hasty footfalls.

"Peter, why are you stopping?" panted John, leaning against the stone of Joseph's tomb.

"John, what if Jesus has been taken, then what?"

Throwing an arm around Peter's shoulder, John whispered, "We'll face it like everything else, Peter . . . together."

John squared his shoulders, releasing his grip on Peter. "Come on, Peter. Mary, are you coming?" he said, heading for the tomb's opening. He paused, then ducked to look inside and shook his head.

Peter had grabbed hold of his courage and charged past John, straight into the tomb. A moment later both men stood looking around. There lay the burial clothes, still sticky and reeking of myrrh, but the cloth from around Jesus's head was folded and laid to the side.

"John! John, do you know what this means?"

"Can it be true? Didn't Jesus tell us this is how it would happen?"

"Now what do we do?"

"I don't know. All we know right now is that Jesus isn't here," John said, rubbing his forehead.

"Well, let's head back to tell the others, and try to figure out what to do next."

Completely forgetting that Mary had been trying to keep up with them, the disciples left the empty tomb and started home. Silent and entrenched in their thoughts, neither one even noticed her as she stood just outside the tomb.

Out of breath, Mary tried to call out to Peter and John, "Peter? John? Where are you going? What about Jesus?"

She must see for herself. What had they seen? What had they seen that seemingly left the men dumbstruck?

Steeling herself, Mary paused and leaned against the entrance to the tomb for a minute. Finally, she could wait no longer and looked inside…

BIBLE REFERENCE: John 20:11–16 The Passion Translation

12 she saw two angels in dazzling white robes, sitting where Jesus' body had been laid—one at the head and one at the feet!

13 "Dear woman, why are you crying?" they asked.

Mary answered, "They have taken away my Lord, and I don't know where they've laid him."

14 Then she turned around to leave, and there was Jesus standing in front of her, but she didn't realize that it was him!

15 He said to her, "Dear woman, why are you crying? Who are you looking for?"

Mary answered, thinking he was only the gardener, "Sir, if you have taken his body somewhere else, tell me, and I will go and . . ."

16 "Mary," Jesus interrupted her.

Turning to face him, she said, "Rabboni!" (Aramaic for "my teacher")

When was the last time you were at the end of your rope? Grief, disappointment, frustration . . . something interfered with your ability to see the next right step. And then God stepped in with the words or actions of someone that empowered you to meet the challenge head on. How did one person's encouragement make a difference to you?

Here in the Flesh

The disciples of Jesus were keeping it on the down low. Jesus's followers were tucked away in the upper room of an inn. The men were drenched in turmoil by the death and disappearance of body of their teacher.

If that hadn't been bad enough, one of their own, Judas, had been the linchpin in the betrayal of Jesus to the Jewish and Roman leaders. The disciples knew Judas was a scoundrel, but they didn't see that coming. And as furious as the disciples had been, they were still shaken to learn that afterward Judas had called it quits on the short end of a rope.

Jesus's followers could not allow themselves to dwell on Judas's choices, in life or death. So much was now at stake, the survival of Jesus's ministry and of their very lives. They knew what they'd witnessed, the grotesque horror of Jesus's crucifixion, then his body missing from the tomb a couple of days later.

They'd heard Mary proclaim that she'd seen and spoken to Jesus in the garden where his tomb was. They were hoping against hope that it was true, that somehow, some way, Jesus was alive.

But right now, Roman soldiers and supposedly a special detail of Temple guards were looking for the followers of Jesus.

They were considered enemies of the state, whether you were talking about the Roman or Jewish rule. No wonder the men weren't sure which way to turn. Whatever way they went, they were on somebody's hit list.

Reports had trickled in saying the handful of followers were considered subversives trying to undermine the Roman government. Seriously? There were days they couldn't agree about where to eat lunch, much less how to overturn the most powerful force in the world.

The Sanhedrin had managed to finagle the crucifixion, and now they'd caught wind of the missing corpse. They didn't want anybody upsetting their game plan to maintain a choke hold on the Jewish people almost as tight as the Romans. That meant silencing the guys left behind by this preacher, this Jesus.

Tempers were short and nerves stretched to their limits in the closed room.

Suddenly, they heard pounding on the locked door, and voices yelling to be let in.

"Guys! Let us in! It's Cloapas and Levi! We've got news, news about Jesus!"

Peter and James leaned against the door while Peter yelled back to the men on the other side, "How do we know it's you?"

What do you mean, know it's us?" Silence for a minute on the other side of the door, then, "Peter, we were there when Jesus healed your mother-in-law then fixed all of us supper. Remember? Open the door, we don't want to be caught out here!"

"Let them in, Peter," said Andrew. "How many people know about that? Besides, we don't want them outside calling our names and giving us away."

"Okay, but you and Matthew get over here and the rest of you get ready in case it's a set up."

Peter slightly cracked open the door and James grabbed the first person he could on the other side. "Get in here!" James hissed.

The two men stumbled in the door but not fast enough to miss Peter slamming Levi's cloak in it.

"Good grief, Peter! Give a guy a break, will ya?" Levi said, checking his cloak for tears.

John stood up quickly, knocking over the stool he'd been sitting on. "What's the news you have about Jesus?"

"Yeah, it better be good since we took a chance on letting you in," Matthew snarled.

"We've seen him!" Cloapas exclaimed, moving into the room.

"Where did you see him?" "What was he doing?" "Where is he now?" The disciples shot questions at the visitors like arrows.

"Give us a minute and we'll tell you all about it; you're never going to believe this. I can hardly believe it myself," Cloapas told the group of shaken men.

"Could we get something to drink? We've already walked to Emmaus, then followed Jesus's orders and rushed back here to tell you," Levi gushed, looking around the room. Cloapas stood nearby taking a hearty swig of wine.

The men gathered around the two visitors, amazed at the story they had to tell. Finally, Thomas took a step back and leaned against the wall, "I don't believe it. Jesus died, but now you say you had lunch with him? How? That's crazy!"

"Is it really, Thomas?" a quiet, but stern voice asked.

All eyes immediately refocused on the One standing by the door.

"Jesus!"

"Peace, brothers!" Jesus greeted the men.

Jaws dropped. Eyes widened. A couple reached for something to hold onto. No one said a word; shock nearly struck all the color from their faces.

"Friends, it's okay; it's really me. I told you the grave couldn't hold me. Don't you remember?" Jesus laughed. "I can tell from the looks on your faces either you didn't remember, or you didn't believe me." He looked around at each man slowly. "I'm not a ghost. Seriously; it's really me!"

Seeing Thomas looking like he was trying to hide at the back of the group, Jesus walked over to him and said, "Thomas, take a look at my hands, my feet. How do you think I got those puncture wounds? Do you want to see my side where the spear pierced me?" Jesus's voice lowered as he touched Thomas's sleeve, "It's okay, Thomas, it's a lot to take in. I don't blame you for doubting."

Returning his gaze to the rest of his followers, Jesus told them, "I don't mind if you look at me, touch me. It's kinda surreal, but a ghost wouldn't have flesh and bone like I do. Not only that, but I'm starved! I didn't finish my lunch at Levi's house. Is there any fish or bread around?"

The fears about Roman soldiers and Temple guards disappeared, at least for the time being. Camaraderie returned to the small group as they settled in around the low table to share a meal. Their teacher was miraculously back with them and that was enough for now.

BIBLE REFERENCE: Luke 24:35–43 The Message

35 Then the two went over everything that happened on the road and how they recognized him when he broke the bread.

36–41 While they were saying all this, Jesus appeared to them and said, "Peace be with you." They thought they were seeing a ghost and were scared half to death. He continued with them, "Don't be upset, and don't let all these doubting questions take over. Look at my hands; look at my feet—it's really me. Touch me. Look me over from head to toe. A ghost doesn't have muscle and bone like this." As he said this, he showed them his hands and feet. They still couldn't believe what they were seeing. It was too much; it seemed too good to be true.

41–43 He asked, "Do you have any food here?" They gave him a piece of leftover fish they had cooked. He took it and ate it right before their eyes.

Describe a time when you disappointed someone.
How did it affect your relationship?
How was the situation resolved?

Breakfast of Champions

"I don't get it, Peter," Andrew said, tossing nets into the brothers' fishing boat. "First, Jesus meets Mary in the garden, then connects with Cloapas and Levi. Then he pops into our headquarters to have a bite to eat with us, and now we haven't seen him for days."

"Beats the heck outta me, Andrew," Peter answered, gathering baskets to hopefully load fish into later. "Everything I thought I knew has been turned upside down."

"Do you think we'll see Jesus again?"

Peter stopped what he was doing and looked at his brother. "Andrew, you remember that night on the lake when I walked on the water for a minute?"

"More like a millisecond," Andrew laughed. "What's that got to do with anything right now?"

"While I was looking at Jesus, I knew exactly what to do. It's when I stopped looking at him that I got into trouble. I don't know what to do, Andrew. I'm not sure how to go on."

Andrew threw a muscled arm over his brother's shoulders for a brief moment. "I know, Peter, I feel the same way. Surely Jesus will come to us again and give us our marching orders.

In the meantime, we need to put some food on the table and coins in the box for our families . . . so, we fish."

"I guess you're right," Peter shrugged. "Looks like the other guys are already hard at it. We better get going before they catch all the fish."

"Very funny!" Andrew called over his shoulder, shoving their boat into the water as the sun dipped below the horizon.

Several hours later, dawn crept across the sky. Hours of rowing, casting, and retrieving empty nets had taken their toll, physically and mentally. The fishing boats slowly headed for the shore.

Someone on the shore was waving to the exhausted men. "Friends," he hollered, "how was your night's fishing?"

"A total wash-out!" Andrew hollered back.

"Complete waste of time and energy," Philip chimed in.

"A big ol' ditto!" James added.

The face was beginning to come into focus as a familiar voice said, "How about toss your nets to the other side of the boat? I've got faith that you'll catch something. Go ahead, give it a try!"

Something in the tone and authority of the man's voice made John jump up from his seat in the boat and strain to see the man clearly. "Brothers! Look, it's Jesus!"

"What? Jesus?" called Peter, turning to face the shore. "Jesus, it's you!" he cried as he tossed off his outer clothes and sandals then dove into the water.

The man on the shore began to laugh. "Somebody's got to stay in the boats. Remember . . . fishing?" Jesus continued laughing as he headed inland and began building a fire. The disciples joined in with the laughter as they recalled meeting Jesus for the first time under the same circumstances. They were astounded then at the incredible haul of fish they'd brought in after following his directions. This time the men didn't hesitate to do exactly what he told them.

By the time Peter was on shore, the heaving boats were close behind him. Smells of roasting fish and bread filled the air.

"Peter, looks like you and Andrew have plenty of fish; bring a few with you. Nathaniel, James, grab a few of yours, I bet you men are starved," Jesus called to his disciples as he flipped fish and bread on the grate.

BIBLE REFERENCE: John 21:3–7, 9–12 The Passion Translation

3 Peter told them, "I'm going fishing." And they all replied, "We'll go with you." So they went out and fished through the night, but caught nothing.

4 Then at dawn, Jesus was standing there on the shore, but the disciples didn't realize that it was him! **5** He called out to them, saying, "Hey guys! Did you catch any fish?"

"Not a thing," they replied.

6 Jesus shouted to them, "Throw your net over the starboard side, and you'll catch some!" And so they did as he said, and they caught so many fish they couldn't even pull in the net!

7 Then the disciple whom Jesus loved said to Peter, "It's the Lord!" When Peter heard him say that, he quickly wrapped his outer garment around him, and because he was athletic, he dove right into the lake to go to Jesus!

9 And when they got to shore, they noticed a charcoal fire with some roasted fish and bread. **10** Then Jesus said, "Bring some of the fish you just caught."

11 So Peter waded into the water and helped pull the net to shore. It was full of many large fish, exactly one hundred and fifty-three, but even with so many fish, the net was not torn.

12 "Come, let's have some breakfast," Jesus said to them.

And not one of the disciples needed to ask who it was, because every one of them knew it was the Lord.

> *What do you do when you don't know what the "next right thing" is? Do you follow the Elijah paradigm: take a nap then have a snack?*
> *What are strategies you use to regain momentum?*

A Fresh Start

Despite exhaustion from fishing all night, an undercurrent of exhilaration ran through the group of men. The past several days had been an emotional whirlwind. A kangaroo court of a trial followed by the execution of Jesus had shattered the bonds they had shared. Just when their sorrow didn't feel like it could be more consuming, word had come that, by some miracle, Jesus had been raised from the dead.

"Jesus, are you back to stay?" asked James quietly.

"James, I think you know the answer to that question. I've always told you the truth. The truth is I was sent for a purpose, and I've accomplished it. The time is coming soon when I must return to our heavenly Father."

Solemn faces encircled the fire that had cooked their breakfast.

"Jesus, how will we go on without you?" Nathaniel mumbled, twisting the corner of his tunic.

"You'll go on quite well. It won't be easy, and most of you'll follow separate paths from each other. But I've given you the tools you'll need to fulfill God's call on your lives," the teacher reassured his disciples. "Nathaniel, what have you learned during our time together?"

"I . . . I don't know, Jesus," Nathaniel answered, rubbing his forehead.

"Sure, you do. You were pretty doubtful when we met. I seem to recall a crack about nothing good coming out of Nazareth. Do you still doubt I am who I say I am?" Jesus asked, trying to hide a slight smile.

"Of course not! How could I, after all we've seen?" Nathaniel paused and stared into the fire for a minute. "I've learned to have, and use, more faith."

Jesus clapped his hands, "Exactly! All of you have learned the lessons you needed most. That's not to say you don't have more to learn and won't make any mistakes."

Peter's chin rested on his hand, his eyes drooping.

"Hey! Peter, do you think you love me more than your friends?" Jesus asked.

Peter shook his head then sat straight up, "Of course, I do, Jesus, what kind of question is that?"

"Just a simple question, Peter. Serve the weak, Peter, the young, the old, the sick, the marginalized."

"Sure, Jesus, whatever you say."

"Peter, are you sure you love and want to continue to follow me?"

"Lord, I already told you I did."

"Good. I want you to be a strong leader. Can you do that for me?"

"Lord, are you talking to the right guy? You know I screw up all the time," Peter's voice grew softer and softer. "How could you forget my colossal blunder after the soldiers took you from us?" Peter dropped his head to his chest, remorse at denying Jesus hanging heavily upon him.

"I didn't forget, Peter; I forgave. I know you're not perfect. I didn't ask you to be perfect, I asked you to lead. You're still here; leaders don't give up," Jesus told the grieving man, putting a hand on his shoulder. "Let's try it one more time, Peter. Do you love me?"

Peter rolled over onto his knees and knelt before Jesus. "Lord, you already know everything about me, the good and the bad . . . and the weak. But mostly, Jesus, I hope you know how much I love you."

Placing both of his nail-scarred hands on Peter's shoulders, Jesus said, "Give, Peter, give all you have to those who seek to know the way, the truth, and the life I've given you." Jesus gently punched Peter in the arm, causing him to look up. "You've got what it takes, Peter!" Jesus smiled, "Oh, and by the way, **I love you too!**"

BIBLE REFERENCE: John 21:15–17 The Message

15 After breakfast, Jesus said to Simon Peter, "Simon, son of John, do you love me more than these?"

"Yes, Master, you know I love you."

Jesus said, "Feed my lambs."

16 He then asked a second time, "Simon, son of John, do you love me?"

"Yes, Master, you know I love you."

Jesus said, "Shepherd my sheep."

17–19 Then he said it a third time: "Simon, son of John, do you love me?"

Peter was upset that he asked for the third time, "Do you love me?" so he answered, "Master, you know everything there is to know. You've got to know that I love you."

Jesus said, "Feed my sheep.

We are all cut from the same cloth, flawed and needy. Think about a time it seemed impossible for a mistake to be forgiven. What does forgiveness look like whether you are giving or receiving it?

Epilogue

Dear Reader,

Thank you for reading <u>Behind the Halo</u>. My hope is that the stories have encouraged you to consider Jesus in a whole new way. Sometimes it seems impossible to think of Jesus as a flesh and blood person living a day-to-day existence, with all the messy emotions we experience as humans . . . but that's exactly what he did.

Connecting to Jesus has been a very emotional journey for me, and not taken lightly. It's a book I felt compelled to write. Stories and words were carefully considered and prayed over. Sometimes they flew onto the screen, other times they had to be painstakingly chosen. (Thank you very much Merriam-Webster online.) There were days when writing came only through tears. And then there were accounts when I had to laugh out loud thinking that Jesus surely wanted to give his apostle(s) a slap upside the head.

Here's the thing, Dear Reader, it doesn't matter if my brain was wracked with trying to find just the right words. It makes no difference if I was afraid my tears would short out the laptop, or a tumbler of sweet tea would get knocked onto it and fry the whole thing because I got so tickled. **The big thing is you. Yes, you!**

I want desperately to give you an inside track on this guy named Jesus who went through the same kinds of hot messes with people *and circumstances as we do. Whether in spite of, or because of that, Jesus still chooses to come alongside us here and now with empathy and compassion.*

And perhaps, Dear Reader, you want to take this new connection to the next level. After considering the human side of Jesus, maybe you want to get to know more about his divinity. It's easy to take that first step; it starts with a simple prayer.

> *Dear God, I see Jesus is more than the man behind the halo; He is your Son. I want to know more about him and how he can interface with my life. I know I've made mistakes and my life could be lived better. Forgive me for those mistakes. Thank you for sending Jesus to connect with me so I can connect with you. I'm asking you to move into my life and show me how to be the person you created me to be.*

Dear Reader,

While all the fictionalized vignettes in Behind the Halo *are based on the four gospels in the* Bible's *New Testament, several different translations have been used. Word choice, in terms of visual imagery and emotional impact, can vary significantly between translations. The online resource, BibleGateway.com, provided easy access to the translations during the writing process.*

Contemporary English Version	Copyright © 1995 by American Bible Society
Good New Translation	Copyright © 1992 by American Bible Society
International Children's Bible	Copyright© 1986, 1988, 1999, 2015 by Tommy Nelson™, a division of Thomas Nelson.
The Message	Copyright © 1993, 2002, 2018 by Eugene H. Peterson
New Testament for Everyone	Copyright © Nicholas Thomas Wright 2011
Revised Standard Version	Copyright © 1946, 1952, and 1971 the Division of Christian Education of the National Council of the Churches of Christ in the United States of America
The Living Bible	Copyright © 1971 by Tyndale House Foundation. Carol Stream, Illinois 60188
The Passion Translation	Copyright © 2017 by BroadStreet Publishing® Group, LLC
The Voice	Copyright © 2012 Thomas Nelson, Inc. The Voice™ translation © 2012 Ecclesia Bible Society

www.ingramcontent.com/pod-product-compliance
Lightning Source LLC
Chambersburg PA
CBHW030326100526
44592CB00010B/588